The Diary of

Gilda d'Este Colonna

By Antonino d'Este

A girl of fourteen begins writing a diary and the early entries show her to be innocent and naïve, but the entries expressing her desires for the future are strangely prophetic.

The Diary of Gilda d'Este Colonna
Published 2004

Printed in the United States of America

ISBN 978-0-578-01736-5

Dedicated to my nephew,

Duke Vince d'Este

And his lovely wife,

Duchess Gilda

NEC SPE NEC METU

Crest of the House of Este,

A Princely family of Lombard origin,
That played a great part in the history
Of Medieval and Renaissance Italy.

Motto: Without Hope, without fear

Books by Antonino d'Este

An American Duke
An American Sheik
I'll Tell You When the Night Comes
An American Duke in Italy
Duchinos and Duchessinas
Secrets of a Bounty Hunter
The Real Lucrezia Borgia
Clear the Bridge! Dive! Dive!
Kings without Crowns
The Reluctant Duke
I'll Think About It
The Diary of Gilda d'Este Colonna
Extended Family
The Money Rats
Commoner Marriage
Murder at the Altar
The Dilemma of Love
One Day Before Tomorrow

List of persons in this book

Antonino Vincenti d'Este, the author, and now referred to as The Old Duke.

Antonino Vincenti d'Este, called "Vince", my nephew and my choice to succeed me to the Ducal Title.

Gilda d'Este Colonna, his wife, and who thus became the new Duchess of Este.

Marina, a girlfriend of Gilda's in the same class at second level school. She started her diary at the same time Gilda did.

Diana, also a classmate and of Gilda's, who started her own diary at the same time Gilda and Marina did.

Francesca d'Este Ruta, my niece, and the only daughter of my brother Piero

Marco, Vince's close friend, and co-conspirator in "crime" Because of his trustworthiness, Marco became the family secretary in the United States, and a confidante of the new Duke.

Count Giulio Villano, a friend and mentor of mine, who promised to be a friend to the new Duke.

Senora Danno was the Second level teacher in Gilda, Marina and Diana's class.

Beatrice d'Este, my second daughter and a Professoressa at the University of Bologna

Leonora d'Este, my youngest daughter

Antonino "Terzo" d'Este, my second son, and is the twin of Lucrezia, my third daughter.

Father Luigi, a local priest

Gilda Colonna
At age 14

Foreword

I first became aware that Gilda was keeping a diary was when she left her personal case behind in her husband's old apartment in New York City.

At the airport before we boarded the plane for Italy, she discovered her loss and called first the secretary Marco, then my niece Francesca, to have her case mailed to the Castello in Italy.

It was Francesca who opened the case and discovered among Gilda's personal items, her diary, and thought the contents of it should be known to me. I instructed her to mail the case to the Castello, but address it to me for examination.

I admit it wasn't proper for me to go into her diary without express permission, but I take the right to guarantee that nothing detrimental to the family was written therein, and which may fall into the wrong hands.

She entered her daily experiences, her cares and thoughts, but I could readily see that it was merely the writing of a girl grown into young womanhood, and all quite innocent of any malice.

It would not be of any interest to anyone else, so why publish it? Well, it is so beautifully written, and gives the reader insight into the mind of a growing female, and all the "so important" things that filled her head. This is not a reproduction of the whole diary, but only those pages I thought had merit, for one reason or another.

And now, The Diary of Gilda d'Este Colonna:

My Diary

Gilda Colonna

Twenty April

This is my first entry in my secret diary. My friends Marina and Diana found out that a classmate of ours was keeping a diary, so we thought it a capital idea that we should start one too, so each of us bought a diary, and we made a pact that we would each know what the others had written on the pages of their own diaries.

Marina said that we must be careful not to copy from each other, so that the diaries would be a true depiction of our individual feelings. This we swore to, amid much laughter, and with our heads swimming with all the secrets we were going to enter for all the years of our lives.

First I'm going to write about Marina and Diana. They are my best friends, and we talk about everything. Most of the girls in our class talk too much about boys, but we don't see the sense to all that. We talk about them but not too much

Since boys are rather stupid, we can't waste too much time on that subject, but we do marvel at all the silly things they do. We can't understand why they always have to argue and fight with each other. They always like to show off, but they are also mean to girls. I don't know why they should be. We don't do anything to them.

Twenty One April

I'm wondering if we should have ever started a diary. This is my second entry, and I can't think of anything to put in it. It has been just another ordinary school day, just like yesterday. The only thing different is that one of the boys fell and scraped his arm. He was bleeding and had to go to the nurse's office for a bandage. Silly boy!

We also got a lot of homework, but I finished it before supper. It was easy to do. Marina and Diana are very nice and it's always good to meet them at school

I will say good night.

Twenty Two April

Today the teacher was very angry. Someone, I don't know who, wrote something nasty on the blackboard. It wasn't someone in our class because it was already on the board when we came in after lunch.

Children who do things like that should not be allowed in school. Senora Danno gave us extra homework, which I think is most unfair to us. We didn't do anything wrong.

My father asked me if I knew who did it, and when I said I didn't know he doubted my words. I told the truth and I was nearly in tears when I appealed to my mother to convince my father that I was indeed telling the truth.

She told my father that I was a truthful, and religious girl, and that she believed what I was saying. That satisfied him so he let the matter drop.

I did all the extra homework, so I hope my father doesn't punish me. How could he believe that I would lie? It's all very unfair.

Twenty Three April

Marina says my father is too strict. When she told her father the story about the words on the blackboard and how angry the teacher was, he just laughed at the idea of the teacher being so discomforted. I wish my father could have a sense of humor like that.

Diana didn't tell the story at home. She said she doesn't think it's such a good idea to say too much at home. Perhaps she's the smart one. I must be more careful in the future, but my father asks a lot of questions, and if he wants to know something, I must tell him.

I know he is only looking out for my best interests, but sometimes I think he's too nosy.

Marina and Diana have brothers, but I'm an only child, so perhaps that's why my father is always watching out for me. He likes to hear that my friends and I study our lessons together. He says that that's a good way to learn faster.

There are a lot of things I'm not interested in learning. I don't like history, because of all the dates we have to memorize. And why should we study about all the great Italian families.

There's the history of the Colonna family that my father says we are descended from, and then there's the Sforza family, and the Great House of Este, the Medici and the Malatesta families. I also hear about the Orsini family, who were very mean and ambitious, but not all of them.

Who cares about all the things that happened so long ago?

One May

Sometimes girls can be as silly as boys. Today during recess, a bunch of girls got into a heated discussion about who was the most popular one in school. What a stupid thing to argue about. When one girl said she was the most popular, I told her that it didn't matter because everyone is different.

Some of the girls say they were the most popular with the boys, and one girl said she knew how to be popular with them. She said she let the boys touch her under her dress. What a terrible thing to say, and I wonder if she actually lets them do it.

Diana said that that girl was just a big liar. She wouldn't do a thing like that because Senora Danno would surely find out about it.

I'll bet the boys would like to do that, though. It's one of the stupid things they say they want to do. I wonder why they are interested in something like that. How stupid!

Goodnight, Diary

Thirteen May

I didn't write in my diary for a while because we had relatives staying with us. My aunt and uncle are very kind and brought me a new party dress. I can't wait to show it to Marina and Diana. They won't be jealous, though, because they often get nice clothes too. My cousin Marianna came with them. She is older and didn't say much to me.

My new dress is very frilly and makes me look older than I really am. It's a little large, but I'm expected to grow into it. We don't have many parties, so I don't know when I'll get to wear it.

It's a light blue color with white trim. I put it on and looked into the Cheval Glass for a long time. When I finally do put it on for a party, I'm sure everybody will notice me. Some day maybe even Senora Danno will see me in it, and maybe she'll say something nice.

I can't wait to show Diana and Marina. That won't be right away, though, unless they can come to my house.

Goodnight.

Seventeen May

Diana went to a beauty parlor to get her hair done professionally. All our classmates noticed how special she looked, and she had to tell all the girls about the experience. She told us of a very nice lady who was her hairdresser, and who talked to her as thought she were a grown-up lady. We wanted to know if she would get her hair done there all the time, but she said that this was for a special occasion. Her family will be going to Rome to visit relatives, especially her grandmother.

My mother always does my hair so that it will look nice for school, but she said that someday I will be able to do it all myself. Marina's mother does her hair too. We all agree that someday we will get OUR hair done by the lady that did Diana's. She looks so nice today.

Girls have to care for their hair more than boys do. The boys should at least try to comb their hair more often, those silly creatures! They don't seem to care how they look. Marina says that when she looks at those boys, she can't believe that they will grow up to be nice looking men.

Diana and I agree that it is hard to believe that. I wonder why boys go to school. They never seem to learn anything.

I have to stop writing. I'm filling up the whole page, mostly because I had to cross out a few things that were too mean to say, even about boys.

Good night

Two June

There was talk today about the last day of school, and all the boys were happy about having summer vacation. I wish there was no vacation because I remember the summer last year when I didn't have very much to do. My mother thought it would be a good time for me to have ballet lessons, but my father was against it.

He said ballet classes should start early, and that I had grown too much to start such lessons now. He said I may have piano lessons, but we didn't have a piano, and anyway, I didn't want to do THAT.

So the summertime passed with that kind of discussions, and instead I learned how to crochet doilies. What a waste of time! We can buy nice doilies at the store if we need them.

I took some drawing lessons too, but I'm never going to be an artist. The instructor could see that quickly enough.

So what will I do THIS summer? The whole thing is such a bore! Well, anyway, the last day of school is not here yet. I think the boys started that discussion. Of course THEY will have a lot of fun, playing ball, or just running around chasing each other. Are they really part of the human race?

Four June

I just can't believe that the boys are still talking about summer vacation. They are making all kinds of plans, and as I suspected, they are planning to play football all summer long.

What can be so exciting about kicking a ball? And all summer long, too! They have to be simple minded, that's all there is to that.

The girls are not making summer plans. We have to wait until we see what our parents want to do. One girl says her family is going our to their summer place in the countryside, where her father grows grapes and other things. She said they do that every year, and her father makes wine and spaghetti sauce from the tomatoes they grow. She has to do a lot of the work, too.

I don't think I would want a vacation like that. It doesn't seem like much of a vacation at all, especially if they do the same thing every year.

I would not want to do any farm work. Marina and Diane agree. Imagine getting your hands so dirty after you were so careful doing your fingernails so that they will look nice.

Ho-hum! There's another school day tomorrow, with more math, history and geography and so forth.

Five June

Today was so embarrassing for me. The subject was the history of the Colonna family, and the teacher Senora Danno, told the class that I was an Aristocrat.

Everyone was looking at me, and I could feel my face blushing, and I even felt my whole body blushing. Then Senora Danno asked me to stand in the front of the class and tell them about my family.

I didn't know what to say! I wanted everyone's approval, so I said that my family did not live like the Colonna family in Rome, and that I was just a plain girl like every other girl in the class.

I also told them what my father had told me. The Royalty of the Colonna family is no more. All that is just history now and the Grand Palazzo in Rome is now a museum and is open to the public.

What I did not know then is that the Palazzo is now under the umbrella of the Duke of Este. It was part of the dowry when the Duke married Laura Colonna.

Luckily, Senora Danno saw my embarrassment and told me I could return to my seat. It was all so awful! Am I special in some way? I don't feel special, but every girl likes to think she will be special some day.

The lesson went on, and we learned that the Colonnas were a powerful noble family of Rome, but that their lives were spoiled by a feud with the Orsini family, who wanted to be more powerful than the Colonnas were.

The lesson will continue tomorrow, I wish I didn't have to go to school,

Six June

I thought about telling a lie and saying I was sick this morning and that I could not go to school, but it's not right to lie, so with some trepidation I walked slowly to school, but I wasn't late.

The great feud between the Colonna family and the Orsini family brought about much pain and sorrow during the Renaissance. The fighting was over power and influence. How stupid it all sounds.

The Colonna family produced one Pope, Oddone Colonna, who became Pope Martin the Fifth, two Cardinals and many other important leaders.

I was proud to learn that one of the Colonna ladies, Vittoria Colonna, was a close friend of the great artist Michelangelo Buonorati, and helped that man in many ways, especially when he was sick. She must have been very nice.

I wasn't so embarrassed today, even though my classmates were glancing at me at times.

I'm going to ask my father if I will be a great lady some day, like Vittoria was, but I won't ask him tonight.

This idea led to a discussion between my friends and me on what we are going to do with our lives. None of us really knew, but we agreed that we could make up our minds when we go to the University.

How can I become a great lady! I'll sleep on it!

Seven June

We continued our studies on the Colonna family, and Senora Danno said we would start our study of the Orsini family on Monday. Well, I'll be glad to change the subject, but I fear the name of the Colonnas will come up again and again because of the great feud between them and the Orsinis.

Tonight I asked my father if I would one day be a great lady, and he asked me why I was thinking about that. I told him about Vittoria Colonna, and how she befriended Michelangelo and is now know in history as a great lady.

He smiled and kissed my forehead and said that I was already a great lady. He said that to him I was a Princess. Fathers are so strange. I know I'm not a Princess. He sometimes even calls my mother his Princess, and she's not a Princess either!

Sometimes I think my father is not completely sane. He is nice to us and to everyone who comes to visit, but he gives me the feeling that he can be a very severe man.

One time, a man who works for him came to the house about some business or other, and my father was quite stern with the poor man. I felt bad for him, but after he left I was too timid to ask my father why he treated the man that way.

There are nights when my father is preoccupied with his own thoughts, and at those times my mother and I know enough to leave him alone. He can sit through dinner and not say a word on those tense nights. At those times my mother barely says anything to me, so we just eat, and that's all!

Eight June

There was no school today, but I was able to go to Diana's house, and Marina met us there. We made sure all our homework was done, and we talked about the things we put in our diaries. They both had some interesting entries, mostly about school, their families and boys!

Diana had the whole story about her trip to the beauty parlor and the way she wrote about it was interesting. She said that a lot of the ladies talked about their husbands, and they were not always complimentary, and sometimes they would roar with laughter, but she didn't understand what was so funny.

Maybe I don't want to grow up too fast, if women behaved like that. I never hear my mother say anything mean about my father, not even when he's in a bad mood. I'm going to be like my mother.

Marina really loves her parents. She has two older brothers, and her parents treat her more special than they do them. Her brothers are close in age, and they really get rough with each other, and at those times Marina feels afraid that they will hurt each other, but they never seem to somehow. At lest they don't show any sort of pain. Maybe they are just being manly.

I told them I'm going to write something about Vittoria Colonna when I learn more about her. I asked them if they ever thought about becoming a great lady, but they said they didn't, and they advised me not to be pretentious.

Still, I'd like to be a great lady, and people can read about ME in the history books.

Nine June

Today is Sunday, and we went to church. I didn't sit with my parents because I saw Marina and Diana and asked if I could sit with them. My father said I could and seemed relieved that I was not going to sit next to him. I know he thinks I'm too restless in church.

My friends and I have the same prayer books that have hard, curved covers with a picture of Mother Mary on them. She looks so beautiful with her hands clasped in prayer, and her eyes looking up to heaven. It is very inspiring and we think of emulating her, and also the Nuns we see in Church.

Father Luigi read the Missal and then gave a strong sermon on the family. He railed against parents who do not set a good example for the children, and then firmly told the children to be obedient. He gave examples of everything he said, like parents who drink too much wine, and mothers who are careless with their speech and may be given to gossip.

He warned about God's wrath if children answered their parents back, and lied to them. I don't know about the adults in church, but I was getting scared not only about his words, but also with the way he was being so forceful, almost shouting at times. I wondered why he was so firm. He seemed almost angry, and maybe something happened in the Parrish to bring this about. We had never seen him like this before.

Ten June

When I got to class this morning there was a lot of excitement, and no one was doing any schoolwork. Senora Danno had to leave the classroom several times and people were chatting about something serious that happened to a girl in another class.

Then Senora Danno gave us our math class, and before we could start history she had to leave the room again. When she returned, she looked distraught, and when she started teaching about the history of the Orsini family, she seemed stressed and disinterested.

Still, we were able to learn that the great House of Orsini produced THREE Popes and many other leaders. I was tempted to ask why the Orsini and the Colonna families were at odds, but Senora Danno had a very sour face, so I didn't ask.

I never found out. I don't think it's enough to say that they were competitors. There was enough room in the big city of Rome for both families to have everything they wanted. At least that's the way it seems to me.

Before school was out there was a rumor that a girl was being expelled from the school, and was being sent to a Convent School for Wayward Girls, but no one knew why. My father always said that I must never repeat rumors, but I can't help writing this in my diary.

I told my father about one of the girls in school being expelled, and all he said was that I should remember the unfortunate girl in my prayers. Did he know something?

Eleven June

Marina started to tell me another rumor about the expelled girl, saying the girl was naughty, but I stopped her, telling her that we must not repeat rumors, and that someday we will hear the truth about her. I wish I hadn't stopped her, but my father is right, rumors should not be spread because they may not be true, and no one wants to be the victim of false rumors.

He reminded me that the Commandments tell us never to bear false witness. He said that girls must be more careful than boys because they tend to be overly curious about rumors and tend to talk too much. Is he being unfair again? Well, I must admit that my friends and me do talk a lot.

I am learning that there are many differences between boys and girls. A little while ago my mother talked to me about the menses, which is such a strange thing. This was after I told her about how Senora Danno was teaching about personal hygiene, and at the end of the school day she dismissed the boys and told the girls to remain in class.

She told us about how to care of ourselves when the menses started. (Author is translating: Gilda used the word "mestrui" in her diary.) I wondered why the boys had to leave, and when Marina, Diana and I were walking home I mentioned that and they laughed at me.

Diana said that boys don't get "the curse", as she called it. Well, I didn't know! It's all so embarrassing and confusing. They made me feel like a dunce.

Twelve June

My mother has been very close to me lately, and she has been explaining how a young woman should take care of herself, especially when bathing. She has been saying some very strange things. Sometimes she says things that contradict each other. I am supposed to clean my feminine part very carefully, but I must not linger there!

How am I supposed to clean myself thoroughly there without lingering there? I told her I wished I was a boy, but she told me not to say silly things because boys have there own special problems. Human beings are not designed very well, it seems.

I have not been talking about this to Marina or Diana because I don't want to look stupid, but one day I did have to ask them about what problems boys have, and Diana, who has a much older brother, said that boys have to clean there too, under a thing called the foreskin, or else they get "cheesy". We laughed at that, and I guess it's better to be a girl after all.

Diana seems to be very knowledgeable about the human body, which should not surprise anyone because her mother is a nurse. She said that she reads her mother books and some things in there are very scary. She began describing some diseases, but Marina and I asked her to stop. It was all so unbelievable and disagreeable.

I'm not so sure I want to grow up.

Thirteen June

Once again the rumors started about the girl who was expelled, and I was tired of people speculating about what great sin she had committed, so I raised my hand in class and asked Senora Danno if she could put these rumors to rest by telling us what really happened.

She didn't answer my question, but she said what my father often says to me when I ask certain questions. She advised the class to put it all out of our minds and think about more pleasant things. How are we supposed to learn about life if we get that kind of advice?

My mother says that there's time enough to learn about things when I get older. She said I shouldn't think too much. What does THAT mean? Is it any wonder that my two best friends and I are confused sometimes?

The older I get, and the more I hear, it seems most people are not aware of the contradictions in life. They go along accepting things that just don't make sense.

Father Luigi, our confessor, preaches that there is only one God, but he's split into three parts. This is called the Holy Trinity, and it means that there's The Father, The Son, and the Holy Ghost. We recite that when we make the sign of the cross.

But we only see images of Jesus in paintings and statues, and the great painters sometimes paint images of God into the pictures. But nobody knows what God the Father looks like, and no one even paints images of the Hole Ghost. It doesn't make sense!

Fourteen June

My father chastises me when I ask questions, and tells me that The Trinity is the way it is, and to take it on faith. He further said that if I didn't have faith, it would be a bad thing, and that I would be led astray.

I complained to my mother that I'm going on Fifteen, and no one is going to lead me astray, but she said that there are many sly tricks that people play upon the unsuspecting, and that I'd better listen to my father.

I asked Marina if she heard of any sly tricks, but all she could think of was the time a boy tried to kiss Diana on her lips, but she turned away just in time and he kissed her cheek instead.

We went to the zoo one day, and there were a lot of people sitting on the benches there, and one young couple were kissing and kissing each other on the lips. They didn't seem to care that people could see them doing it. We agreed that kissing a boy was a private thing and no one should be seen doing it.

Then we laughed and said that we didn't want any boys kissing us anyway. They never brush their teeth! That was funny to us, but secretly we knew that we would let a boy kiss us if we really liked him, but that's ALL!

Then we stopped laughing and wondered what we would do if a boy wanted to put his hand up our dresses, and we said that there was nothing else to do but slap his face and tell Senora Danno.

Fifteen June

I didn't say anything to my friends then, but I felt it would be a pleasant sensation if a boy touched me there. Then I felt ashamed, and decided to confess to Father Luigi that I had an impure thought.

When I saw my friends today, I told them of my strange feeling, but Diana said that I didn't do anything wrong because it was just a girl's curiosity and that's not a sin. Marina disagreed and said it was indeed an impure thought, but how can we not think of it once we said it?

No, Father Luigi will have to tell us what to do. I think that if we talk about such things it will only lead to impure thoughts, and God know all about it when you have one of those.

I asked my mother how I could avoid impure thoughts, and she said I should just not think about them. Is that an answer? I suspect that my mother doesn't know the answer so she just dismisses it. My father does the same thing.

We have to confess to the good Father Luigi and do our penance. Then God will forgive us and cleanse our souls. Yes, that's Father Luigi's responsibility. I must not ask Senora Danno. She must teach us our lessons, but sometimes she tries to help us with problems too.

Things are getting complicated.

Sixteen June

Sunday again and after Mass, we got permission to go to the park. Diana's big brother Ricardo had to walk with us and make sure we were not bothered by anyone. I heard my father ask him to be extra alert, reminding him that I was of noble birth. So! The truth came out! My father never spoke directly to me about that.

I liked walking along the pathway in the park and couldn't wait until we got to the zoo. Some of those animals seem so ferocious that I'm glad they're inside those strong areas and can't get out.

I saw a woman reaching over the fence and putting her hand close to the bear's cage. I don't know if she wanted to feed him something, but he quickly reached his paw through the cage bars and slapped her hand. She didn't act like she got hurt, but she must have.

Ricardo, Diana's brother, treated us to a nice lunch after we saw the zoo animals, but I was disappointed in not seeing any young couples sitting on the benches kissing each other on the lips. I didn't say anything to my friends because Ricardo was there, but I will tell them later. I wonder if they were on the lookout for the same thing. Girls will be girls!

Then a girl friend of Ricardo's came walking along, and they greeted each other, but I had the feeling that if we weren't there, they might have kissed each other on the lips. I sensed that because of the way the looked at each other, and how they smiled in a way that suggested that the shared a secret.

Seventeen June

Since it's getting close to the end of the term, my father said that we're going to do some interesting things during my vacation. One thing he said was that he's going to take us to Rome to see the Palazzo Colonna. He will get tickets, and we'll be able to see the inside!

I asked him why he never took us before this, and he said that I wasn't ready for it yet. He can be so strange, at times. I was ready last summer. At lest I think I was, anyway. What could he have meant by that?

Well, the important thing is that he says I'm ready now, so whatever that means, it's a good thing. I'm going to tell my friends and maybe my father wouldn't mind taking them too. What a time that will be. We can all see how the Colonnas of Rome lived during the High Renaissance. It is a magnificent Palazzo. The Orsini family did not own anything like it in Rome.

I must say I love my father. I don't always understand him, but he's a good man. I'll have to ask my mother how they met. It will be a good thing to know for the future. I know that if a man comes to my house to ask for me, my father will have to give his permission. If it happens that he doesn't like or trust the young man, then he will turn him away.

It will not matter if I like him. My father has the final word and I will not go against his decisions

Eighteen June

The school term will end in about two weeks, and Marina and Diana and I are already missing each other. We don't live very far apart, and we can easily walk to each of our houses, but still, it's not like meeting in school every day during the week. We must find things to do together, now that we're almost fifteen. We should be able to go to the cinema now, if we promise to stay together at all times.

Another sad thing is that now that we're getting older, we will have to give up our childish ways, and we'll have to accept more responsibilities. It only makes sense that we do that.

My mother has been hinting that there will be more duties for me in the house, and I may be entrusted with going to the market. Along with all that, we will have to start thinking about going to the University soon, too. There may be time yet, but time flies by, so we have to think about things. At least that's what my mother is saying.

It may be my imagination. But it seems that even Senora Danno is treating us as though we were older already. Even boys are talking to us more, and one nasty boy said that we are filling out and starting to look sexy! If we are growing, that's certainly none of his business, so he'd better keep his eyes to himself. Well, I guess that's a dumb thing to say.

Oh my! We'll have to start going to women's stores for our under things. All this is happening to quickly for me.

Nineteen June

There was a stranger hanging around the school who appeared to be interested in the young girls. I didn't see him but he was reported to the police, but was gone before they arrived. I told my father, and he was incensed. In fact, I don't ever remember my father being so agitated. He made arrangements to change his work hours at his office so that he could escort me to school and back home.

This did not only affect me during school hours but he restricted me to the house even after school. He even made time to patrol around the school, saying that the police were fools and lazy, so he patrolled the area trying to find any man who fit the description we had.

My mother and I are frightened, because we do not know what my father intends to do, and also, what if he accosts the wrong man?

Fortunately, the excitement died down after a time, and my father resumed his regular hours at the office, but he had a worker escort us to and from school. The other girls were being escorted too, so it was still a reminder that there was what might have been a bad man hanging around.

He was never caught. Some people said that he may have been a passer-by and not a bad man at all. I don't think we'll ever know, but our part of the city is not a place where strangers would just pass through, unless they were driving their cars.

Fortunately, the whole issue did not interrupt our lessons, so we learned more math and history and other subjects.

Twenty June

Even though the weather has been getting quite warm, we had to make sure we were properly covered as we walked to school. Our arms had to be covered and our skirts well below the knees. Our shoes and socks had to be proper, and even our undergarments were not to be the scanty kind.

Imagine that! And just who will be checking our underwear? Now we see another example of the difference in the way girls and boys are treated. The boys did not have any regulations, at least not that I know of.

My friends and I had a long discussion about that and could not come to any real conclusions. Marina said that girls had to be protected more than boys, but she wasn't sure why. Maybe it's because everybody considers us the weaker sex. They should see us in the gym!

Diana was sure of one thing. Boys are much stronger than we are because of their big muscles. She told us how her oldest brother would pick her up and hold her over his head with one hand, then walk around laughing as she begged him to let her down.

She said that when he works with her father, she could see that her brother is just as strong as her father is. It is her brother that is walking her to school these days.

Marina agreed that even her brother, much younger than Diana's, is quite strong, and found it easy to move heavy furniture.

Twenty One June

This is the last week of the school term, and things are getting lax in class. Senora Danno told us that we will have her as our teacher for one more term, and then we will be going on to the University. We were glad to hear that because she is a good teacher and kindly to everyone, but she is especially aware of what the girls in the class need.

Of course she could be very firm when she had to be. We didn't get away with anything.

At lunchtime I brought up the subject of the boys being physically stronger, and I made the argument that, well, I though we're stronger in other ways. It's easy to be strong when you have big muscles but certainly girls are smarter. Marina and Diana didn't have a problem with that

Then I asked Diana if she thought Ricardo was on kissing terms with the girl we met in the park. She said she had no idea, but that it wouldn't surprise her. After all, she said, Ricardo was of that age! Hmmm! When are girls of "that" age?

Twenty Two June

Dear diary, this is the way Marina starts all her entries in her diary. She says it makes her feel she's talking to an intimate friend. I'm going to try it and see if it works that way for me too.

We went to school today, but it was hardly a regular day of study. Senora Danno did go over some of the lessons, but she was short and brief. I can't remember all of the subject matter she talked about, and she did not give us any homework. It's almost as though the school term has already ended. I'm not complaining. An easy day at school is most welcome.

She gave us some examples of the kind of math we will need over the summer, like shopping, pricing and making the right change for customers if we work in a shop or some kind of business. Then she told us that we had to dress in the right way so that people will take us seriously.

In history she once again mentioned the Orsini family, but spoke at great length on the Renaissance period. She pointed out that there was a great surge of art and artist of all kinds, but there was also much fighting and intrigue.

I'm glad she didn't mention the Colonna family. I hope nothing will change anyone's attitude towards me, now that it has become general knowledge that I am "High Born", whatever that means. I was born like everyone else, and my mother is just a homemaker.

I can't remember what else Senora Danno talked about.

Twenty Three June

Today was much like yesterday in class, except that many of the students didn't come to school. They may have thought that the term was already finished, but they will be marked absent, and that will go against their record. They are being foolish.

Senora Danno spoke to us more intimately. She told us about her life in respect to her deciding to become a teacher. It was quite inspiring and some of the girls said they would like to be teachers too.

It was a most relaxing day, and Senora Danno showed her loving and caring side. She warned us that the next semester would be harder than the past one, and made us promise to concentrate and work even harder on our lessons.

She told us how hard work was very rewarding, and that it was the best way to live a better life. We had to promise again that we would strive and not slacken or allow ourselves to be distracted.

She was very emphatic on that point, telling us that there are things that will be distracting, but that we had to ignore them. When she wagged her finger at us and said that we should only allow those distractions into our heads, and only when we got married we would understand what she was aiming at. We couldn't help giggling, but I'm not sure what we were giggling at.

Twenty Four June

Tonight at dinner I asked my parents about when I could start thinking of marriage, and my father shocked me when he said that I should not think of my marriage at all. HE was the one who would decide when, and with whom I will marry. When I asked why, he told me quite loudly that I would be able to marry only a noble man and that I should put any other thoughts out of my mind.

I'm feeling sad tonight, diary. How is a noble man going to find me? I don't know of any noble men, and now I will never get married. My father said HE will think about it, but what can HE do about it? He doesn't know any noble men either; At least I don't think so.

What will my friends say when I tell them this horrible news? Should I say ANYTHING? It may alienate them from me as though I were some new kind of different person. I may lose my best friends. What misery I'm feeling tonight.

Now I know that my father can never be a fair man, and I shall have to suffer. Shall I NEVER marry? Will I have to go into a convent? I can't think anymore and I can't write anymore.

I shall put my face into my pillow and drown the noise of my sobs. I may as well die.

Twenty Five June

I started crying again when I met Marina outside of our classroom. I could not help my tears, but Senora Danno overheard me and came and to console me.

When she understood why I was crying she told me that my concern about marriage was not the real cause of my tears. I didn't understand her, so she immediately added that I was crying because I was making the transition from a teenager to a woman.

The three of us went to the teacher's lounge and she explained that certain hormones at my age could make my emotions become unbalanced. In other words, I just became very unsure of myself, and my father didn't understand that it wasn't really that I wanted to get married. I just needed emotional assurance, and I sought it from my parents.

Well, I was reassured by this wonderful teacher and went to class with a happier spirit. Then as I began to think again, and I wondered more about the marriage issue. How is THAT going to be solved? I didn't feel like crying again but I had to understand all that better. I think I deserve an answer.

A word from the author:

Dear Reader, I'm taking the privilege of using artistic license to cover a gap in the diary caused by repetition and omissions during her summer vacation. I wish to inject here that the two families, the d'Este and the Colonna, have been historically intertwined. My own wife was Laura Colonna, a distant cousin of Gilda's

Senorina Gilda Colonna did make entries about her visit to the Palazzo Colonna in Rome, and of some of the things she learned to appreciate about her family's history. The following is a condensation of her entries during that period. Note the change in her writing and thinking as she approached her fifteenth birthday.

Dear Marina,

I guess everyone is happy that the term ended and the summer vacation began. There were many good-byes and promises to keep in touch, and soon all the students were in their own homes. I'm sure their minds were filled with all the things that come with a vacation lasting several months.

Within the week, my father kept his promise, and took us to Rome to visit the Palazzo Colonna, and other sights in the Eternal City He did not want any one else to come on the trip, so I'll write to you as often as I can.

It may not be easy for me to make entries in my diary every day, but you must keep your entries up so that I can read them when I get home. Also keep the cards and letters I send so that I can be reminded of what I wrote to you, and

I will be able to fill in the gaps and explain more than in the writing what it all means.

When we got to Rome we went to a nice Pensione and settled in for the night. Of course we went out to dinner first. You will not believe how crowded Rome is. There are so many tourists. We are not used to that many people moving around and competing for taxis and restaurant tables.

The next morning, after our Prima Collazione, (Breakfast) we went directly to the Palazzo Colonna, and my father went to buy tickets that would allow us to go in, but someone there recognized him, and they let us join the group of tourists that were to follow the lady guide without the need of purchasing the tickets. I don't know how they knew him, since he rarely visits Rome.

The lady guide introduced us to the group of tourists and they wanted to speak to us because we were Colonnas, and they asked if my father was a Prince or a Duke. He explained that he was descended from the Colonna Princes, but had no title of his own. I could see that they were disappointed. I think they wanted to be able to tell the people back home that they met Italian Royalty.

It was at that moment that I wished I had a Royal Title, so that people would be impressed. How great it would have been to tell them that I was a Princess because my father calls me that, but I would have looked foolish. I know that I'm a girl of fourteen, and I tend to have grandiose dreams, but I just feel so strongly that it would be so nice to be a Royal lady.

Well, we're all going to be fifteen by the time school opens again, so maybe by that time I'll be more mature and I won't have impossible dreams anymore.

The guide was giving us some history of the family, and we saw portraits of our ancestors. They looked so nice and healthy, but they sure wore funny clothes. The gowns on some of the ladies were magnificent, though.

On the first floor of the Palazzo we walked into a room that was so incredibly decorated that one had to blink several times in order to believe one's eyes. Every detail of the room, from floor to ceiling was evidence of great artists. The guide pointed out some of the family crests, and I asked my father if we could adopt one and paint it in our apartment. He just smiled lovingly at me.

The lady was mentioning a lot of names of Popes, artists and architects, but I can't remember everything. I do recall that part of the Palazzo was not built by a Colonna at all, but was build by Cardinal Giuliano della Rovere, who later became Pope Julius the Second.

Later, the part that he built was taken over by the Colonnas. Did they buy it, or just take it? That's a mystery, at least to me.

Then there was fighting, and two of the Popes tried to destroy the Colonna family, but later, Pope Pius the Fourth returned all the property to Prince Marcantonio Colonna the Second, and this led to the rebuilding of the Palazzo that we are seeing in the present day.

Pope Pius the Fifth also proved to be a good friend of the Colonnas.

Our guide said that this building is one of the last remaining of the great Patrician residences of Rome. I realize that Senora Danno could not have taught us everything about the Colonna family or even the Orsinis.

On the ground floor antechamber is a Baldecchino dominated by the Colonna coat of arms. We are told that the art treasures collected by the family were at one time scattered, stolen during the French Revolution, which caused so much confusion in Europe.

The British were the greatest thieves of all, which is why so much Italian art wound up in London. Looking at the collection now, I feel that much of it is primitive, but then I can't say I know much about fine art. Still I can't understand what the fuss is all about.

You should see all that is here now. There is so much fine furniture, beautifully and so intricately carved, and there are marble mosaics on the floors and so much tile work all around.

The frescos on the ceilings and all the molding work surrounding them are so magically blended, and one gets dizzy trying to see it all and remember it all. In fact, one cannot see and appreciate everything in one day.

I asked my father if we could come again tomorrow, but he said we had other marvels to see in the city, and in Tivoli. I asked him what was in Tivoli, and he wondered that I didn't learn about Tivoli in school. If we did, I can't remember it.

The Palazzo Colonna and its contents span several centuries, and I'm beginning to feel a sense of pride and belonging. Does that sound strange? Remember, I don't want our friendships to change, so don't judge me, all right?

This place, according to our guide, is more about history and art than about the Colonnas. There are so many rooms that one must have a map to find his way around, and, and each one decorated differently. You'll see stuccoed walls, canopies, statuary, and lovely window treatments. There are also base-relief carvings everywhere, and the frames and trim are magnificent. It's hard to imagine such riches all in one place; It's truly a movable feast!

Finally we visited the garden, and I will leave that to your imagination. Try to picture in your mind huge and magnificent stairways, and clever pathways snaking among the fountains and trees.

Your friend,

Gilda.

Dear Diana,

Today we took a rather long ride to Tivoli and we visited the famous Villa d'Este. Senora Danno said that when school starts we're going to study about the d'Este family, and now I will be able to tell the class what I've seen here.

We didn't have a guide here as we did at the Palazzo Colonna, so we just walked around, my mother and I following along behind my father who acted as our guide. As he told us about the marvels of the villa, some tourist began to follow us to listen in, and they even began asking my father questions about everything.

I must say I had no idea my father was so knowledgeable about the villa and the d'Este family, but then, he did study them at one time, and may even have visited the villa before. I assume he did because he seemed to know his way around all the paths, and the terraces.

My mother smiled at me when we saw how much my father was enjoying telling the crowed about how the hydraulic engineers designed all the waterways so that the fountains and waterfalls would work the way they do. The big trick was to bring all that water here in the first place.

He seemed to forget for the moment that we were his family, and we merged into the crowd and just followed along. I wish I could remember all the technical things he was saying about the construction of the villa, but I don't have a good memory for such things.

I hope I remember enough to make Senora Danno proud. You know how her eyes light up when one of her students knows his work well enough to talk about it.

Diana, the Castellino here is not as large or as sumptuously decorated as the Palazzo Colonna, but the gardens are here are probably the best in the world. Once again I experienced that light-headedness that comes when a person is newly surprised by such magnificence.

My father told us that the Villa d'Este here at Tivoli is listed as a world heritage sight. It is a masterpiece of both Italian architecture and of garden design. Don't laugh at me, but as I waked around I began to feel more like a d'Este than a Colonna. Remember, a distant cousin of mine, Laura Colonna, is married the present Duke of Este the one they call "The American Duke".

I may sound silly about feeling like a d'Este, but when you come here you will want to become as one with the Villa just as I feel now. You'll see! You just can't help it. This must be what heaven looks like. I can just imagine Jesus showing us around the heavenly gardens as our guide.

I'm beginning to like history more and more. The best way to study the past is to visit the sights where history was made. Of course that's not always possible, but that's all right, because once you catch the spirit of history, then the rest comes easy. At least I think so.

Today is my fifteenth birthday, and I'm sure I will never again have a birthday like this one. I have been going through so many different feelings that at times I feel almost breathless. After we leave the Villa d'Este, my parents are going to give me a special birthday dinner. Too bad we can't be together.

Cardinal Ippolito d'Este, the son of Alfonso the First, Duke of Ferrara, and the Duchess Lucrezia d'Este Borgia built this Villa. She was the illegitimate daughter of Pope

Alexander the Sixth. The Cardinal built this place to be close to Rome whenever a Pope died. He had to live close by because travel was so difficult that many Cardinals didn't get to Rome in time.

I don't know where to look first. All the fountains, cascades, troughs, and pools are all working at once. And they make a very pleasant noise.

I'm collecting cards and slides of the place I'm seeing, and I'll be able to show them all to you, Marina, and the rest of the class.

After we left the Villa and returned to Rome, the restaurant we went to had prepared a birthday party for me. Everyone was so nice, and the cake had "To the Princess Gilda." on it. I was blushing, but I was proud too. Then a group came and sang "Happy Birthday" and I had to blow out the fifteen candles.

What a day! I'll be glad to get some sleep.

Your friend,

Gilda

Dear Marina,

You must read the letter I sent to Diana. I told her all about our visit to the Villa d'Este in Tivoli, and after that, about my surprise birthday party in Rome. I missed you both, and I think it's too bad my father didn't want to take any of my friends on this trip.

During the party, I asked my father if he would take us to see Pompeii, but he reacted very strongly and said I must not ever see that place until I was married! What does seeing the ruins of Pompeii have to do with marriage? Sometimes I worry about my father's sanity.

Can you make any sense out of that? Well we did go to see the Trevi fountain, and my mother and I tossed coins over our shoulders and into the water. When you do that you have to make a wish, so I wished I would some day marry a very important man. My father asked my mother what she wished for, but he didn't ask me.

That was lucky for me, for I didn't want him thinking that all I had was marriage on my mind. How often do you think about it? Do you have any idea what kind of man you want for a husband?

The Trevi fountain is build between two buildings and is up against the wall of one of them. It's quite large, and I don't think it's very pretty. When we stopped for lunch at the Piazza Navona, I saw the Bernini fountain right in the center of the piazza. Now that's beautiful!

After lunch we went around to the Pantheon. My father wanted to spend a lot of time there, so we were able to hear about it from the guides that took groups around and spoke all kinds of languages. Pantheon means "Many

Gods" but now they hold Catholic Mass there. That's why it is also called The Church of Saint Mary and the Martyrs.

The measurements of the interior are of a giant ball, with the ceiling being the right size at the top, and the imaginary ball would touch the floor. At the very top is a hole called the Oculus, and it is the only source of light in the building proper.

The tomb of the great artist Raphael is here. Imagine being so important that you can be interred here!

This building is that last complete example of ancient architecture. It looks nice, but also a little strange. Still, I'm glad it's there and that we had a chance to visit it.

Tomorrow we'll go to the Coliseum.

Your friend,

Gilda

Dear Diana.

Today we visited the Coliseum and you will not believe how large it is. I understand that it is still the largest stadium in Europe. It is truly an awesome place, and I would have liked to have seen it when it was newly built.

As marvelous as the building is, one can't imagine the carnage that took place here. My father is telling us about the games and the fights, and he's acting like he's just reciting history. It's as though all that bloodletting was just an incident, instead of a period of mass murder and horror.

He said that five hundred thousand people were killed here, and over a million wild animals. Think of the madness of the people who enjoyed all the fright and hopelessness of the victims. They had to be mad. Certainly the Emperors were madmen

I tried my best not to listen to my father, but I seemed to be able to hear the anguished cry of the Christians who were killed here only because they were Christians.

I don't know what my father's plans are for tomorrow, but I was glad to get out of the Coliseum! I began to feel something like terror in my own soul. God forgive us all.

Your friend,

Gilda

Dear Diana,

What an experience being in Rome is. Today was church day. My father took us to a little church called Santa Maria Della Vittoria, and I was surprised at how small this church is, and how extraordinarily decorated it is too. We came here to see the incredible statue by Bernini called "The Ecstasy of Saint Teresa"

I'm sure you've seen pictures of this and some of the other marvels that I have been writing to you about but believe me; you have to see these treasures in person. That's when they almost become unbelievable. I'm glad my father didn't rush us today because my mother and I wanted to look at this statue for a long time.

He said that tomorrow we would see more of the work of Bernini at the Villa Borghese museum. Bernini did so much artwork that you can find samples all over Italy and beyond. That reminds me! We don't live too far from Modena, I don't think. What do you say that we try to take a daytrip there and visit the d'Este Museum and the family Archives in the Galleria Estensi.

We will see the huge castle the Duke, Francesco the First, built there, and the city itself that is beautiful too. In the middle of that castle is a courtyard where they rode horses, training them and parading them. Imagine that!

Bernini carved busts of many famous people, but the largest one he did was of Francesco the First d'Este, Duke of Modena. I understand that the Duke was so pleased with the bust that he paid Bernini as much money as the artist got for carving the fountain of The Four Rivers in the center of the Piazza Navona that I mentioned in a previous letter.

There I go talking about the d'Este family again! It is so strange that I should be coming across that name again and again. I wonder why this is. Somehow that name is hidden in my heart.

We started going to another church, but stopped off to see an island in the middle of the Tevere. (We call it The Tiber River.). We were able to walk across an old bridge and go to the point of the island and watch the water flow by. It was very relaxing.

Then we drove across the Tevere into that area of Rome called Trastevere (Across the Tiber River.) and went to a small church called "Saint Cecilia". There, built into the altar, enclosed in a glass case is a statue called "The Martyrdom of Saint Cecilia", by the sculptor Stefano Maderno.

He was twenty three at the time he did it, and it is said that he carved it after he saw the corpse of the Saint. I don't want to believe that. I want to believe she was alive and praying to the Lord.

Diana, can you believe that looking at a marble statue could tug at your heartstrings? Like looking at the statue of Saint Cecilia, I was moved by the agony depicted there in that case. How she must have suffered, and how well the artist captured her in her throws of misery.

We went to an outdoor café for lunch and then went to see the church of Santa Maria Maggiore. Once again my eyes were treated with such beauty all around me. It just surrounded us and we walked and walked, admiring everything. My father didn't say anything. He must have thought that the church could speak for itself, and I have to agree with that.

In the center of the church is a statue of a seated Mother Mary, and the church itself does not have a main altar, but rather a series of altars, so that many masses can be said at the same time.

And guess what! Gian Lorenzo Bernini is buried right here! I think it's wonderful that so great an artist is honored this way by the church and his nation. He deserved all the homage being paid to him.

We spent more time there, much of it looking at the painted panels in the ceiling. There must be thousands of them, one more beautiful than the last. Both my mother and I complained, facetiously, that we developed cricks in our necks.

It was a long day and we were happy to go to dinner, then to our Pensione. (Author's note: A Pensione is a small hotel, usually on one floor of a commercial building, and also usually run by one family.)

The building was located on the Piazza Esedra, also called the Piazza Della Republica, and has a very large fountain called The Nyaid fountain in the center.

Usually traffic goes around this fountain, but on this night there was a street show going on, so we listened to some of the singing. Many people were dancing and the whole scene seemed so spontaneous.

An odd thing happened as we stood there in the street. A man came and stood next to my father and started talking to him. I saw my father getting very angry and said something in an angry voice and the man moved away. I didn't dare ask what that was all about.

What a day, and what a night!

My father said that we'd better get some rest because tomorrow was going to be another special day. He didn't say, but I could tell he was saving the best for last. I did some writing but I had to get some sleep. Really!

Your friend,

Gilda

Dear Marina,

   We had coffee and a roll for breakfast in the Pensione dining room, and then started out for the Vatican. Imagine! The Vatican!

   We drove over the bridge that has all the angels on each side also carved by Bernini. There are times when I get the idea that Bernini did everything, but of course he didn't.

   There, as large as life is the Castel Sant'Angelo, the fortress that some of the Popes used to hide in when there was serious trouble in Rome. We went in and saw the papal rooms and the strange place where the goldsmith and sculptor, Benvenuto Cellini, was imprisoned for embezzlement, a charge that was proven false, and guess who had him released! Cardinal d'Este! There's that name again!

   We went into Saint Peter's square, which is a funny name for it because it isn't square at all. The curved colonnades on each side were designed by none other than, you guessed it! Bernini! And notice, Marina, that the word colonnade has our name in it. What a coincidence!

   The Vatican is a city all by itself. It has its own government and everything that a government does, like making its own stamps and its own laws.

   Entering the great doors of Saint Peter's Basilica is unbelievable, and the first thing that catches your eye is the beautiful while marble statue of Jesus and Mother Mary called "The Pieta" by Michelangelo.

   Then, as you walk further in you realize that you are in the largest cathedral in the whole world. There is a modern statue of Pope Pius the Twelfth, and there are huge sculptures of whole groups of people. As we walked down the center aisle, my father pointed to measurements on the floor showing the sizes of lesser cathedrals of the world. Then we arrived at the Baldecchino, a large canopy of bronze over the main altar designed by Ta Dah! Bernini! It stands over the main altar of the Cathedral.

Bernini must have had a great sense of humor. If you go close to the twisting columns of the Baldecchino you'll see insects crawling around. And one fly looks so real you almost want to swat at it, except that it's clearly made of bronze.

The top is made to look like canvas, and the hanging leaflets seem to be moving in the breeze, just as a canvas top would do if it were out of doors.

How did Bernini find the time to do so much of the work we see? He must have had helpers. I doubt one man could have produced such a body of work alone.

In my opinion, that's one of the mistakes Michelangelo made in his carving. There is so much of his work that was left undone because he wanted to do it all himself. Luckily he realized he needed helpers when he painted the Sistine Ceiling, otherwise that would have been left unfinished too, I suspect.

One story is that Pope Julius the Second kept after Michelangelo, asking almost every day when it would be at an end. The great artist was said to have answered that it would be at an end when it was finished.

And then there's the dome! Looking way up you'll see letters saying something in Latin, and these letters look like the might be three feet tall. Guess again! They are NINE feet tall.

Near the very top is a walkway with a railing and you can see people up there looking down at the people below them! We must look so small to them, and they look small to us. They had the courage to go way up there. I would not have that kind of courage. The thought of it makes me shiver.

We went behind the back altar and down into the basement and saw some of the glass-topped caskets of some of the Popes. The must have been very small men. They look that way anyway.

We had to go out into the street and around the Vatican City walls to get to the Sistine Chapel. On the way to the chapel itself we saw part of the Pope's living quarters, and the mural that shows the picture of the very beautiful Lucrezia Borgia. She looked like a sweet angel.

You'll remember that she became the Duchess of Ferrara when she married the Duke Alfonso the First. I wish I could be HER! Do you think that's silly?

By the time we left Vatican City and got to our Pensione, I was sure we would be going home in the morning. But no, my father had yet another surprise up his sleeve. He was having a good time surprising his family I wonder if my mother felt the excitement I felt during our visit. She certainly didn't show it.

Your friend,

Gilda

Dear Diana,

We started out this morning for the Baths of Caracalla, an ancient set of buildings built by that Emperor for the use of the people of Rome. There are two things remarkable about these ruins. One is the size. As we stood on the floor of one of the baths that was still partially intact, the ceiling was at least three to four stories high. What a great thing it must have been in its time.

The second thing is that they hold full operas there in the summertime. I saw the stage that was built among the ruins and there was plenty of room for the crowds that came to see the operas. Wouldn't it have been nice to have lived in those times when Caracalla ruled? I guess not. We may have wound up in the Coliseum as food for the lions.

Still, how very spectacular things must have been. When no one was looking I bent down and took a nice black stone from the floor as a keepsake. It wasn't a nice thing to do but some of the pebbles were loose, so I'm sure other people took souvenirs for themselves too.

Well, I was naughty, but I felt good about it as I rubbed the stone in my pocket. No one would miss it, and I did think it was pretty. I'll give it a nice home and I think the Lord would smile at me.

After lunch we went to the Palatine Hill, and had a good vantage point to oversee the old Roman Forum. Just think, the Emperors and the Generals walked those streets. I saw tourist down there but we didn't go. There was only one small building left from the old forum, and that was the Temple of the Vestal Virgins.

I asked my mother if they were truly virgins, and she asked me what I knew about such things. Actually not very much, but I knew that when a woman got married she wasn't a virgin anymore, so it's easy to figure that puzzle out. I think.

We went to the Via Veneto to have lunch at an outdoor café, and this is where all the stars and other important people come to be seen. I thought we were dressed very nicely for this place, but there were people there that were showing off!

The ladies had jewelry and long gloves and hair fixed in such a way as to make me laugh. They looked so strange. Even some of the men looked funny. I didn't know anybody, and no one looked at us.

Afterward we went to the Villa Borghese museum. This place was once a private home, and I can tell you, I could live in a place like that! It had a strange elevator that could only take one person at a time up to the second floor.

The big surprise came when I saw the large collection of sculptures, and most of them were by, yes! Bernini again! I think these were his very best. They certainly are his most famous.

There is the magnificent statue of Apollo and Daphne, showing how she began turning into a tree as he captured her. You see her toes growing roots into the ground, and her fingers growing twigs and leaves. The work is so delicate that I reached over and touched it with my finger to see if it was real, but a guard yelled at me for doing that.

My father gave me a stern look.

Then there was one called The Rape of Persephone, and where the man was holding her, you could see his fingers indented into her skin. Such accuracy!

Then the other world famous statue was the one of David getting ready to throw the stone at Goliath with his slingshot. The twisted motion of his body made one think he would move at any moment.

We also looked around at the other works of art. There is the reclining figure of Venus Victrix, by Antonio Canova. I don't know who that lady was, but she must have been an aristocrat.

We drove by the Victor Emanuel Monument, but we didn't stop, as we went by my father told us that the stature of the former king was much larger than it looked. The whole thing was made of white marble.

It is called the Vittoriano, but American visitors call it the Typewriter and some Italians do too.

We are starting home tomorrow. There is no doubt about it this time.

Your friend,

Gilda

Dear Diary,

Home again, and I'm glad! The trip to Rome was very exciting and interesting, but now I think I'll just rest for the remainder of my summer vacation. I'll go to see Marina and Diana as soon as I can. And we can compare notes on everything. They will want to hear my stories, but I'm sure they have stories too, if I know them.

Right now all I want to do is sleep, sleep, sleep! But before I drift off to the land of slumber, I'm going to think of myself as a grand lady, along the lines of Lucrezia Borgia.

The first thing I'm going to do is ask Diana and Marina to go with me to Modena to visit the d'Este Archives. That's where the bust of Duke Francesco the First is on display. Of course I'll need my father's permission, but I think he'll give it to me because he's been treating me like I'm a big girl lately.

We will be able to see the portraits of some of the d'Este family there as well, especially the one of Ercole, Duke of Ferrara, which we see in our history books.

I don't think my friends will share my enthusiasm, thought, because they don't dream of the things I dream of. I do so want to be a great lady. I will pray that it will happen.

Good night/

Dear Diary,

I think I'm losing my friends. They didn't want to hear of my adventures in Rome and just complained that they had to stay close to home. I asked them what they did during the time I was away, but they didn't want to talk about it.

I don't think I should be angry with them. They were bored and disappointed, and maybe a little jealous. I still want them as friends, though. I don't know what I'd do without them, especially at school. I noticed that when I told them I tried to get my father to take them to Rome with us, they seemed to feel better about me.

I forgot to mention my idea of a trip to Modena. Maybe they will want to do that. It will be a great adventure if we could go on our own, but I know we'll have to take Diana's big brother if we go.

Marina's birthday is coming soon so maybe we can use that as an argument to go. It occurs to me that I'm the oldest one of the three of us, so maybe I'll start thinking of myself as a big sister. No! I don't think that will work out too well.

I'm going to mention the trip to Modena to my father first, so that there won't be any disappointment later if he refuses. I'll ask him if he thinks I'm growing up, and maybe I'll try to butter him up so that he'll be agreeable.

Do girls have an easier time getting along with their fathers than boys do? It doesn't take much thinking to conclude that boys have it easier. At least it would seem that way.

Dear Diary,

I must ask my friends if they put dates on their diary entries. It would avoid confusion if I did that. I was forgetting that. The advantage of not putting days in is that when you skip a few days it isn't so obvious. I don't think I'll date them as I make my entries, but maybe not. It's not that important, and anyway, I'll know when whatever I put down happened. No one else has to know.

Some diaries come with all the dates printed on the pages, but I think that's wasteful. It means that if you skip a few days all those pages are wasted. I'm glad we bought the cheaper ones.

I asked my father if we cold go to Modena, telling him that we were interested in going because of our schoolwork. He hesitated, but asked my mother's opinion, and she said that we had to promise to stay together at all times, even when we had to do personal things.

I guess that means we all have to go to the toilet together too. That's going too far! No one likes to listen to toilet noises, but I had to promise, so we'll just have to do the best we can. At least we have permission to go. I know that Marina and Diana will not have any trouble because their fathers are not as strict.

Now the only thing we have to do is decide on a date. There is still plenty of vacation days left, and I only hope my friends will have enough interest in going. History is not their favorite subject, but I can tell them that we can have fun too.
Good night.

Dear Diary.

It is all set! We're going to Modena on July fourteenth, but now to make hotel reservations. We don't have to worry about transportation because my father is going to drive us, and then he'll pick us up when we're ready to come home. We don't have to take Diana's brother either.

We're going to be free for several days, but I'd better not abuse this privilege or I'll spoil things for the future. When you're fifteen years old, you have to learn how to get around your parents, although I think they know we will want more freedom as we get older, and are preparing for that time.

I can't think of sleeping while planning what else we can do in Modena besides seeing the Museo Estense. I should not have to think too much about it, actually. Imagine! Three fifteen year old girls out on their own for the first time! We'll think of something, that's for sure!

Maybe we should talk to Senora Danno about our trip. She can tell us what we should be looking for in the Archives, and also what to do in dangerous situations. I don't want to be one of those smart kids who think he knows everything when I don't know every danger that may come our way.

We have to be careful. Tragedies happen when the innocent fall for the wiliness of the clever, my father says. Truthfully, we girls don't want much. We'll go walking and go to restaurants and order what we want like grownups do, and maybe we can visit the Castello there.

Dear Diary.

Senora Danno was very helpful. She recommended that we ask to see the actual letters written by such important people as Isabella d'Este, who the Senora called the First Lady of the Renaissance. She told us about how intelligent Isabella was, and said we will be studying about the House of Este when school starts again.

I told my friends that we'd better pay attention to all this so that we'll be ahead of the class when we go beck to school, but they laughed at what they called my folly.

Sometimes I don't understand them. I think that's a good idea. I told them that we're going to find our studies much harder, so we'd better be prepared as much as possible. What's the matter with them? They seem to be so lethargic these days.

My mother gave me another talk today. She told me I had to be very careful in Modena. She warned that it isn't always what we girls do wrong, but that a bad person may notice you and do something wrong. She gave me some signs I should be aware of, but it all made common sense, so I know what to do to avoid it.

It worries me though. Why should some people behave that way? What do they hope to gain from doing wrong things? It's all so confusing, but she said it has something to do with their minds being twisted. She further said that they have courses in the University that teaches the human mind, and what can go wrong with it.

That's fascinating. Imagine learning about human thinking! I'm going to ask about that.

Dear Diary,

Well, I found out why my friends have been acting strangely lately. Diana has become enamored of a boy that lives in her block. She said she was going to ask her father if she could go steady, but the boy hasn't said anything to her yet!

She said he was one of the older boys, and was totally handsome. Marina pointed out that it made more sense if the boy noticed Diana first, and that she'd better not ask her father about going steady yet.

What do you think Diana did? She stopped him on the sidewalk and talked to him. He was polite, but wasn't sure who she was, so she told him her name and where she lived and kept blabbing even as he tried to go about his business. She walked him all the way to his house and he finally had to tell her he had to go in.

Then she said she would like to meet his family! I think she's letting her emotions rule her head. He told her that maybe she will meet his family some day, and she understood that that meant he was interested in HER!

I told her it didn't mean that. Marina agreed with me, but she was adamant. She's heading for trouble if she doesn't come to her senses.

What troubles me is not only that Diana is losing her head, but also that Marina knew about it and didn't tell me. That hurt my feelings.

Dear Diary.

I asked Marina why she kept Diana's situation a secret from me, but she explained that I was so busy talking about Rome and Modena that she couldn't get a word in edgewise. That could be true! I am a bit of a chiacarone! (That means a chatterbox, Author.)

Diana wants us to hang around her block to catch a glimpse of her "boyfriend", but we pointed out how silly that is. We girls shouldn't hang around like that. People can get the wrong idea. Then, he's really not her boyfriend. He's probably forgotten about her already.

Marina told Diana that she'd better wake up to reality, but again Diana resisted the advice of her friends. What good are friends if you don't listen to them? She wants to go to his house and knock on the door, and introduce herself to his family!

She is pazzo over this boy! Marina told her that if she did that, the boy will be embarrassed, and would have to explain to his family that he has NOT been playing games with young girl's affections. This can even cause trouble between the families.

Maybe she'd better talk to her mother or Father Luigi. Either one will point to the error of her ways.

The boy's name is Giuseppe. Joseph in English, but she calls him Peppino. Look out Peppino! Diana wants to get her hooks into you!

Dear Diary,

I spoke to Diana again today, but I didn't go into her infatuation with Peppino. Instead I talked about our trip to Modena again, and that we should all be ready to go at the appointed time. She agreed.

Luckily Diana didn't act on her impulses to go to Peppino's house. It may have sunk into her head that we were right. On the other hand, she may have decided that there was time for her to insinuate herself into his life since he lived right on her block and wasn't going anywhere soon.

Whatever the case, she started acting normally again, and Marina said it might have been a temporary aberration. The one disturbing factor in all this is the idea that it could happen to any of us girls.

The heart has a way of locking on one boy, and sometimes it takes an earthquake to break the lock. At least that's what my mother said. She further said that we couldn't be blamed for this. Its nature and the heart is a hunter when it is seeking love.

All I know is that it scares me. I didn't like what happened to Diana. A sensible girl was suddenly transformed into a fanged vixen, and it wasn't pretty.

I'm going to pray to Jesus before I go to sleep so that this never happens to me. I have the feeling that Diana, although she is acting quite normally now, will never be the same again.

How sad that Peppino may never know. What would he do if he did know?

Dear Diary,

It was early when we got into the car with our things and started out for the city of Modena. By this time I wasn't the only one who was excited at the prospect of having so much freedom once my father dropped us off at our hotel.

I told the other girls that we should start out slowly and get a feel for the city, but that we should make the Museo Estense our first stop. I insisted that we must not lose sight of the fact that this was supposed to be a study trip, but I could not see the faces of my friends sitting in the back seat.

Well, it was a good idea to let my father hear that we were going to be studious, but I wonder how much we fooled him with that. He didn't gain his place in the city government by being easily taken in.

Someday maybe I can be as wise as my father is. He is the best one I can learn from when it comes to matters of real life. Also, I may be able to get a good job through him when I graduate from the University. That is, if my dreams of being a great lady don't turn out.

It took quite a while to get to Modena and we had to stop several times along the way. My father understood that females have to visit the toilet more often then men do, and with three of us in the car, he was not surprised or annoyed when one of us called for a stop.

Modena is not too far from Bologna, so we may as well get used to the trip, since we plan to go to the University there..

Dear Diary,

We all skipped a day making entries into our diaries because getting everything settled into our hotel room took a lot of effort. Afterward my father took us to dinner, and then he gave us some precautionary words, and then left for home.

I could see that he was worried, and didn't like the idea that his only child was being left in a city she didn't know, and in the company of two young girls who weren't much wiser.

Well, the chicks must learn to flap their wings and fly sometime, so he knew he had to take the chance. It was all part of raising a daughter. Still, he didn't like it. He didn't like it one bit.

So here I am on the second night in the city and thinking about my parents. I must never disappoint them. I prayed to Jesus that I never would. Together with Marina and Diana, we prayed for guidance.

Tomorrow we will definitely go to the Estensi Museo. Today we just walked around and looked at some of the attractions of the city, the home of the great Pavarotti, and we went to the old Cathedral where he and his father used to sing. It had a strange interior construction. It was not like any of the Cathedrals I ever saw before. Everything looked so old.

Well, it WAS old! What could anyone expect?

I asked my friends if they were glad they came, and the said they were, so it was a good idea after all.

Dear Diary,

What a wonderful place the Estense Museo is. When we saw the bust of Duke Frederico the First we were just amazed at the intricate carving. We all had comments about the intricacy of the hair, which you might expect from a bunch of girls.

I didn't know the painting of Duke Ercole of Ferrara was so huge. How fierce the Duke looked in his armor and with such a scowl on his face. Just think, Isabella and Beatrice d'Este grew up with this fierce man, and Lucrezia Borgia had to learn to live with him after she married Alfonso.

I would have trembled were I in their place. We all agreed that we were happy our own fathers were such benign and nice looking men. Still, Duke Ercole must have had a soft side. We'll learn that when school begins.

I didn't forget that we had to ask about the important papers held there in the archives. A folder was placed in front of me on the table, and I was told it contained many of the original letters written by Isabella herself.

I ask permission to touch them and received it after promising I would handle them gently. I felt a thrill go through my body when I held in my own hand a letter from Isabella to her eldest son.

She actually wrote this letter in her Studiolo in the Castello of the Gonzaga in Mantua. What beautiful handwriting and what lovely paper. I promised myself that I would pay more serious attention to the way I write anything in the future.

Dear Diary,

We had to go back to the Estense Museo for a second time to see the rest of it. We didn't want to miss anything. I a courtyard open to the street there were large carvings they were just placed there without any order and looked very old.

Unfortunately, on this visit, a man approached us and said he would like to be our guide and show us around the city.

I remembered my mother's waning about sly persons trying to pull tricks on the unsuspecting, so I told him we were not interested. The problem arose when he refused to take our refusal for a final answer, and the situation was made worse when Diana said that maybe we could use a guide.

He really became a pest after that, and kept following us around. When we finally got outside he began to tell us of all the places he could take us, for very little money, and that set an alarm off in my head. If he was offering us a bargain, then there had to be something up his sleeve.

I finally found my voice and began yelling at him to leave us alone. People waking by stopped to look, and this finally served to tell the man he'd better get a move on.

To make sure he didn't follow us, I hailed a taxi and told him to take us to our hotel. I will always believe that the man had bad intentions, and I was very firm with Diana for giving him the idea that he had an advantage.

Marina agreed that we had to learn to keep our mouths shut in front of strangers, and Diana could see the sense to that. We were lucky today.

Dear Diary,

This afternoon we decided to go to the cinema, but when we got there the signs on the marquee showed pictures of nearly naked women in poses that left us in no doubt that we didn't want to go in there.

We walked to the town square and saw some nice statuary on the center strip of the main road. Then we looked into the display windows of some fine shops but we all agreed that everything was too expensive, and anyway, we didn't have that much money on us.

When we got back to the hotel we decided that it was time to call my father for the ride home, but when I called I was told that he couldn't come for us, and that we would have to take the train. We asked at the hotel desk in the lobby about the location of the train station and the man was very helpful.

We went out for dinner, and when we got back there was a policeman waiting for us. I was told that my father called the Police Department in Modena and arranged to have an officer put us on the train for Monza.

We quickly packed our things and got into the police car. We all laughed when Marina said that she wondered if the people who saw us getting into the car thought we were being arrested. Even the young policeman laughed.

Diana found the policeman very attractive and said so. It didn't take much to have her forget her handsome Peppino! Marina and I looked at each other as if to say that Diana was one girl that had better marry soon

Dear Diary.

Last night my father picked us up at the train station and drove my friends to their homes. When we got home my mother hugged and kissed me as though I had been away for years. That told me something about motherhood that I would keep in the back of my mind...

My father was all smiles at the motherly scene; then he began asking me questions. So many questions! When I told him about the man who pestered us at the Museo, his expression turned grim, and I was sure he'd never let me go out like that again.

Anyway, it was good to be home again, surrounded by all the familiar things, especially in my room. Still, I knew in my heart that I would want to travel again soon. It was fun in the main, and I believe the person who said that travel broadens the mind was right. Somehow I felt smarter; more experienced.

Then I began to feel a little unsettled. I could not understand the reason for this and decided to talk to Marina and Diana if they had the same experience. I'm not sure, but it seems that when a person comes home again from traveling, he's never the same again.

Had I changed in some way, dear diary? Was there something about this trip that came home with me? It must be so, because even as I prepare for sleep that feeling would not leave me.

What was it? Did the trip somehow make me older? How strange life can be. At this moment I don't know my own mind.

Dear Diary,

At least I know now that I wasn't being fanciful last night. When I spoke to my friends they admitted that they had the same feeling that something in their lives and their thinking had changed forever.

Marina laughed and said we shouldn't worry. She was sure that we grew up a little, and that we were going to go through many such shaky moments. She added that girls do, but boys do not.

I asked her how she knew that and she said that her brothers seem to grow older physically, but not mentally. Marina can be so funny at times.

Diana mentioned "her" Peppino! Here we go again! We told her to be careful, and she assured us she would be, now. I sure hope so.

I was also right about my father's grim expression. He said that I had enough traveling for one summer, and that now I must stay close to home and be a help to my mother. I know he loves me and worries about me, so I certainly can't disagree with him. It makes me feel good to know that I'm his "little girl", and that he would always guarantee my safety.

There's no argument there! I want to be safe, too. I hear about other children who have bad thing happen to them. My parents always say that children have to be watched at all times. I may be fifteen, but it's a big world, and I know I'm not ready for what it has to offer yet.

Dear Diary,

I have the feeling that I'm going to become quite adept in the kitchen, and also at the market. When I went there with my mother to shop, she showed me what to look for in fresh fruits, vegetables and meat. I had no idea that there was so much to it.

Then cooking was another thing. I knew a little but now that my mother was teaching me how to be on my own in preparing meals, I realize that there is more to that, too, than I ever thought.

My friends are not learning all this yet, but I told them I thought it was a good idea if they started to pay attention to what running a home is like, even though we were preparing to become professionals

After all, even professional women have to know how to cook for their families. If I become a great lady, I will still need to know about such things, I suppose!

My father has started to give me a regular allowance. He said that I now must learn how to control my own money, especially since I'll be going to the University in Bologna next year.

I hesitate to tell my friends because I don't know if they will be getting allowances as well. On the other hand, if I do tell them, maybe they can convince their parents that they should learn how to control their own money. If I need to learn this, then the same applies to them...

I'll tell them! They also have to be certain that I'm always open with them. This is how good friends should behave toward each other.

Dear Diary,

The summer is passing so swiftly, and we'll be back in school in no time. I'm not worried about that, except that Senora Danno told us it was going to be a much harder year because we're preparing for the university. I felt that the past year was hard enough, but I'm trying to convince myself and my friends that we're up to it.

We'll continue studying together, and we should have a way of doing our work more efficiently. Another thing is that this year we will be getting information that will guide us into what courses we want to take. This is designed to lead us into choosing our professions.

I anticipate going back, but I'm apprehensive about how well I'll be able to do. We have to keep up our grades if we are to make it to the University. Sometimes I think that growing up is not such a wonderful thing. I know that's silly, because we can't stop growing.

Actually I notice that Marina and Diana are growing up in certain ways. And I think I'm filling out too. Everybody in school is going to notice too, so I'll bet the boys will make more remarks than ever.

What am I worried about? The boys have to grow up too, so maybe they'll have more sense this term. I'll also bet that they will be asking some of the more mature girls to go steady. Oh, yes, diary, some of those boys will get to "that age" when they will want to kiss girls on the lips.

I wonder what that feels like!

Dear Diary,

Diana says that she wants to start being kissed on the lips. She says she is going to encourage that from the boys because she feel she needs to know how to kiss when she meets the boy she wants to go steady with. She says she's ready, and it's time for all of us to do it.

I asked her what she would do if the boys want to go further and she said that maybe we're old enough for that too. That made Marina get angry because she said we have to maintain ourselves for marriage.

I'm not going to let any boys kiss me on the lips, and they certainly will not get too familiar because I'll warn them that I'll tell my father. Marina says that's a good idea. Yes, let the boys know that the will face punishment if they are disrespectful.

Marina also said we have to watch our reputations, and that argument convinced Diana that she had better think about being good. She agreed that being mindful was the best way to live in the long run.

Thanks to Marina, Diana came to her senses. There will be time enough for us to do all the things grown women do when we get married. We laughed when Diana said that she'd want to do all the wild things people hint at. She said there must be things married people do that we don't even know about.

I wonder how true that is. I know I'm naïve, but there's nothing wrong with my imagination. That, and my mother has been telling me about self-care, that hints at what is on the way. Maybe I want to grow up faster now.

Dear Diary,

It's only weeks now before we start school. My father insists that I start studying now. Well, I don't have the new work but he said I have to review the old work, which I have not paid any attention to during the summer. He's right, I did not do any reading, and I remembered that there are things I have to prepare.

After dinner I settled down with a book about the Great War. History gets awfully depressing when we have to read about that conflict. I cannot understand what the reason for it all was, but my simple thinking tells me that such things have to be avoided, I see no reason why so many people have to be killed, and at the end of it all nothing is really solved.

My father came to my rescue. Even though he told me to study, he decided that we should sing some songs, so he told me to put down the book and we started singing. Many of the songs from southern Italy are so nice and the words are so meaningful. Sometimes they are so sad, too.

"Santa Lucia Lontana" is one of the sad ones, and tells about someone who is far away from his home and seeking his fortune, but misses his home so much. We hadn't finished singing it when there was a knock on the door, and the lady who lives next to us heard the singing and came to join in.

She has a nice voice, and made a good fourth to our little musical ensemble. Afterward my mother made a desert for us, and we chatted for a long time. I'll have to read tomorrow. In fact Id better start even before breakfast.

Dear Diary.

I could not get the sad words of that song out of my mind, and wondered how it would be for me if I had to leave my home and live far away. I wondered if we would be filled with sadness when we went to live in the dorms of the University. I know it's not the same thing, but its still being away from home.

Marina and I went over to Diana's house to study, but we started talking and didn't do much studying. We talked about being away from home, and Marina said she would miss her parents, but Diana said she would be comfortable in the dorms.

She admitted that she would feel a little homesick, but not too much because she was sure we were going to be very busy and distracted. She pointed out that life at the university would be different from anything we had known before, except for the trip we made to Modena. She feels that was good preparation.

I don't know about that. In Modena we didn't have books, classes and professors. Diana may be right is some ways though. We will have to make our own choices with very little guidance. Yes, we will have more freedom, but also more responsibilities, so we'd better be prepared.

A good way to prepare is to talk to Senora Danno about it. She should be able to tell us how to live there and what to do to acclimatize ourselves to our new life.

We all agreed that was the thing to do. I wonder how Senora Danno will feel about it.

Dear Diary,

Time is beginning to hang heavy on my hands. For all purposes our summer vacation is over, and we're back to study, study, and more study, and school hasn't even started yet. My father said that we would be ahead when school starts. He was sure that far too many of the other students will not have studied at all during the summer.

He made the point that school should be taken seriously because at this time of our lives, that was our only job and our only responsibility. I think he is right. Our parents do everything for us for all these years, so the least we can do is show respect by studying and knowing our lessons.

It really feels like our vacation is over now, because my mother took me to stores to buy my clothes for the New Year. I didn't realize I needed so much. I had grown out of many of my things, so I needed a lot of everything.

We had to buy things that didn't show, if you know what I mean. I needed shoes, and boots for the cold or wet weather, and an outer coat. We came home with so many packages, and my mother wanted to get it all unpacked and put away so that my father wouldn't see how much she bought.

It's not that she was being dishonest or sneaky. She said that it was one way a wife takes care of her man, but I didn't understand what she meant. It's a strange world. We even have to change the rules after we get married, it seems to me.

Dear Diary.

I couldn't wait to tell my friends about all the things we bought, and I didn't realize that they were not going to be able to shop for so much new clothes. It's not that they are poor, but that there are other siblings in their houses, so what money came in had to be used for all the children.

This is one of the advantages of being an only child, but there are disadvantages too. Marin and Diana talk about sharing within the family, but I don't have that experience. Maybe it would be nice to have that, and I do think of sharing with my friends. I should think of them as my sisters, but I don't know if they would ever think of me that way.

Ever since it came out that I was highborn, there seems to have been a certain division. I hope I'm just imagining it. Well, it may be a matter of birth, but I don't see any difference between my friends and me in any other way.

Economically we seem to be on a par, and socially as well. We like the same things, and I think we're very comfortable with each other. After all, we've been friends for a long time and are always visiting each other's houses. No, there is no difference between us that I can see. At least not now there isn't.

I makes sense that later in life, as we begin to go our separate ways, there will be differences in every way, but that doesn't mean we can't continue to be friends. Both my mother and my father have friends with which they keep in touch. It will be the same with us.

Dear Diary,

Today I overheard my parents taking about me. My mother wants my father to take us out on a picnic before school starts, and my father readily agreed. I immediately thought to ask if my friends would be able to come, but I heard my mother say that she was sure I would want to ask Marina and Diana to come.

My father said he didn't mind keeping an eye on me but that it would be difficult to keep his eyes on three girls. My mother said that she would make sure the girls stay close together.

When my father ask why she wanted to go on a picnic particularly, she said that we girls saw enough of cities, and that we had to spend time in the country to appreciate nature.

My father asked why that was important and my mother said that we girls needed to see the work of God as well as the work of humans. She wanted to be sure we blossomed in a more complete way.

I smiled when I heard that. Are girls like flowers? You could say that we are in some ways. I'll have to talk to my friends about that. It's funny to hear my mother say things sometimes.

My father must have understood what she meant, because he didn't comment, but I knew he must have been thinking about it. I could not help but think of how much they love me. I makes me feel so warm all over. Are other girls this lucky? I wonder! Some of my classmates don't seem to be.

Dear Diary,

I'm sorry I haven't made any entries for a few days. We went out in the country and me and my friends wanted to run all over the countryside. How exhilarating it all was. We saw some wildlife and almost envied them their freedom, but my father pointed out that most life on this earth couldn't expect to live into old age.

In the wild, animals can be expected to be to be killed in fights, or caught and eaten by predators. How awful! He said that even insects and plants have to learn to defend themselves. He reminded us that we eat our meals every day, and that those meals are comprised of animals and plants that died so that we can eat.

Diana wanted to know if we ate any insects, but she thought she was being funny. Actually, my father said, we may very well eat them. When wheat is harvested to make flour, may insects could be ground down along with the wheat.

Diana said she was going to give up eating bread, but my father laughed. He said that Diana might as well give up eating pasta. I could tell that he was enjoying himself taking to us.

He told us a lot about nature, and then talked about the universe. When we look up into the night sky and see so many stars, he said that we're only seeing the smallest part of the universe, and that there were things out there that we would not believe.

I began to understand better why my mother wanted us to go into the country.

Dear Diary.

When my friends and I got together today we talked about all the new things we learned, and we didn't talk about school or boys. I wonder if I'll ever be as smart as my mother.

We certainly began to see things in a new light, and it all seemed to put school AND boys in a better perspective. There's more to the world and life than those things. But then, how do we all fit into this picture?

Why did God make us the way we are, and why are we here? We learned in catechism that God made us to know him and to love him. That's fine, but why did he need us? If he could create the whole universe, why would people on a small planet be so important to him?

Something is missing here! There has to be a better purpose that that. Besides, he didn't create us the way we are now. Not if we can believe the scientists and the evolutionists. I wonder what's going on.

Diana says that maybe we shouldn't think about all that and accept what things are. Marina then said that we should just go with the flow. The only thing wrong with that is that we'll never understand the big picture, if the is one.

I don't know, diary! If there are things we don't understand, can that be dangerous for us? How do we decide what's important? Is anything important? There must be things that are important, but how can we tell?

I don't see too many options here! Good night!

Dear Diary,

I didn't sleep too well last night. Maybe I had too much on my mind. My mother soon made me focus, though. At breakfast, she reminded me that it was time to prepare for school. We went to the registrar's office and got all the paper work started.

Marina and Diana were there with their mothers. And our mothers chatted for a while. They didn't talk about anything heavy. They just talked about a lot of small things, but somewhere in all that small talk was a lot of hidden meaning, I'm sure. They knew we were listening, so they must have used some code words. Mothers can be funny.

We just listened politely and answered any simple questions that were asked of us, thing like were we happy that school was starting again. We said we were, but how do you honestly answer a question like that? I don't know if I'm HAPPY about it. We're going to school, and that's all there is too it.

Maybe life is like that too. We're going to have to live through it, and that's all there is to it! Marina and I smiled at each other, but Diana was in another world by that time. My guess is that she's thinking about "her" Peppino. Hmmm! Is it possible that she be could really be in love? At the age of fifteen can she be in love?

I think it's just an infatuation.

Dear Diary.

This was the first day of the new term, and the place seemed so strange. I can't believe that this is the same school I've been going to for so long. Yet nothing has changed that I can discern.

Even Senora Danno looks different. She even SOUNDS different. When I told my mother that, she laughed and called me a silly girl. She said that I was the one who changed. I was growing up, she said, and my mind is what's really different.

Can that really happen to me? When I go to the university, I'm going to study about the human mind. It's too fascinating a subject to just sit and wonder about. If I learn how the human mind works, I may be able to tell what everyone is thinking. Wouldn't that be something?

Senora Danno was right. The work we are getting now is much more difficult, and there's even more homework. I don't think we're going to have an easy time of it. But the teacher is helpful in many ways; explaining things she knows are new to us and alien to us.

Diary, I don't know if I'll be able to make entries every day now that we have so much work, I can only do my best to keep a complete record. After all this is the story of my life. If I am destined to become a great lady then my own record will be the best source of information for future scholars.

Maybe I'm getting too conceited.

The author interrupts the daily diary entries once again so that repetitions and omissions may be avoided. In fact, the whole of the year in second level was almost devoid of any reader interest, in my opinion, until it was nearly time for Gilda's graduation and preparation for the university.

There were the usual family issues, the school problems and the near romances based mostly on the fantasies of the female mind. Yes, the boys have their fantasies too, but this is Gilda's diary, so I'll wait to see if anyone wants to write about adolescent boys in Italian schools.

There is one area that may bring a smile to the face of the reader. Diana continued throughout the year to try to attract the attention of her obsession, the boy she called Peppino. The things she did to get his notice I'll leave to the reader's imagination, but they illustrate how far some young ladies are willing to go to "catch" the young man that they want, lest his attention be directed toward another.

Isn't that the way the world works? Isn't it true that in most cases it's the woman who catches the man? Even if men don't believe that, would they change it in any way?

This brings us into the argument for or against arranged marriages, but I've already expounded on that in my book "An American Duke in Italy". It's the story of my own marriage to Laura d'Este Colonna, so I won't rehash it here.

We resume the entries of Gilda Colonna to here diary at the point when her concerns involve her graduation from the second level and admission to the University of Bologna.

Dear Diary.

I have neglected you for so long that I'm almost ashamed to visit you now. However there are many important things to enter on your pages.

It has not been an easy year for the students in school this past year. The lessons were so tough, but some of the subjects were fascinating. We were all taken with the history of the House of Este. We saw a slide show of the Castello Estense in Ferrara, showing the outside, with a moat that still exists, and of the interior rooms, each of which has its own name.

It was all so amazing! To think that this was the home of Duke Ercole, Duke Alfonso and his wife Lucrezia Borgia, and all their children., and the Marchioness Isabella Gonzaga d'Este, and Princess Beatrice Sforza d'Este.

The Cardinal Ippolito d'Este, who build the Villa we visited during my last vacation, also was born and raised here. We can all be proud and interested in our history. What country can boast such a richness of history and personalities than Italy?

Also included in the slide show was the art collection held by the d'Este family. To see so many riches all in one place boggles the mind.

It is easy to believe that this place was the art hub of the peninsular during the days of the House of Este. It attracted the best poets and writers, musicians and actors, making it a boiling pot of artistic endeavor.

When I told my father about it at dinner he just smiled at me lovingly, but said nothing.

Dear Diary.

As graduation gets closer, Marina and I were shocked to learn that Diana would not be going to the university. She has decided to go to nursing school. I don't know how to think about this. Maybe it doesn't mean that our friendship is breaking up, but in one way it does. When Marina and I go to the University, we will be talking on a different level than Diana.

We must make a promise that we will have periodic get-togethers to keep the friendship alive. We have been together too long to break up the team. We studied together and think along the same lines. It shouldn't matter that one of our number is going to study for a different profession.

Actually, even Marina and I are going to study for different professions. I'm going in for Psychology, but Marina hasn't made up her mind yet as to what she will pursue. She actually likes math, so maybe she may want to become a bookkeeper or a math teacher.

We're going to go for our fitting for our caps and gowns. I think we're all going to look nice. The caps and gowns will be the same for the boys and the girls. That seems odd. Why should we all look alike?

When I spoke to Marina about it, she laughed, saying that the thought of boys wearing gowns was hilarious. She was sure that they would all look silly, and that they would be embarrassed.

Dear Diary,

It was a wonderful day. Graduation from Second level is a day I shall never forget. Everybody looked nice, even the boys. The gowns did not look silly on them at all, and we could see that they were wearing white shirts and ties.

Are these the same silly and awkward boys we were in class with all year long? They were quite handsome, I must admit. Their hair was combed, at last. I could see that they were all barbered under the caps.

All the parents were dressed up so nice. Everyone was smiling, even through the speeches that were boring. Senora Danno gave a wonderful speech, saying how proud she was of her student's accomplishments, and was sure we would go on to do great things.

I was inspired because I though a lot of what she was saying was meant for me to hear. I had told her that I wanted to be a great lady, and she said that all things are possible. I honestly feel she was thinking of me when she said certain things, but of course all the boys and girls might think that.

When the graduation exercises were over, I went to hug my parents, and my father's eyes were welling up, and there was a furtive tear going down his cheek. I felt a little pang in my heart thinking that I was the cause of his tears. I know he is very proud of me, but I never want to be the cause of his tears. He seemed so forlorn.

Dear Dairy,

Last night when we got home my parents presented me with a fine wristwatch that must have been expensive. They also gave me an impressive pen and pencil set. My mother had prepared a nice meal for us. Something she knew we liked.

Many of the student's went out to eat last night, but my parents wanted to celebrate at home. Although we are going to have another summer vacation, I think they wanted to be at home with me before I went to the university. I wanted to spend more time with them too, because to tell the truth, I'm a little daunted at the thought of going to Bologna for years.

Marina felt the same way. We were happy to think about it before, but now that the time is here we are not so sure of ourselves. University life is a lot different that second level and we will essentially be on our own.

Whereas before we HAD to study, in the university it is assumed that you want to learn, so they don't press you to study too much. However, if you fail, then out you go! What are we getting ourselves into?

One thing we can feel good about. There are going to be a lot of new students there, so we won't stand out, or look like dummies, I hope

Dear Dairy,

Today my father surprised me by saying that we were going to Ferrara to visit the Castello Estense, the Palazzo die Diamante, and the Palazzo di Schiffanoia. He also surprised me by saying that Marina can come, if her father approved.

I am almost too excited to write this entry. The very first thing tomorrow I will run to Marina's house to tell her and to ask her father to let her come. My father gave me a note to her father, saying that his daughter will be carefully watched. That note will do the trick, I'm sure.

Diana wasn't going to be asked because my father said that this was an educational trip and a preparation for the university, and that now that Diana was going to nursing school, she would not need the history lesson that the trip would teach us.

Still, I think Diana should come. She is our friend, and she will probably feel bad at not being invited. There are times when life presents us with situations that are so touchy. I told Marina that we could make it up to her when we get back, maybe treat her to something, or bring back a gift for her.

All this did not dampen our excitement, though. We were eager to go to Ferrara.

Dear Diary,

Early this morning, right after breakfast, we picked up Marina and went to the train station in Monza. We were more than ready for an exciting day, and along the way my mother had to caution us that we were chattering too much, and to remember that we are cultured ladies.

The train ride was nice, and we arrived in Ferrara in good time. For a moment Marina thought she had lost her luggage, but she found it immediately and her panic was short-lived.

My father hailed a taxi and we went to the hotel where he had made reservations for us a few days before. We got settled in and went out for lunch. My mother insisted that we visit the Cathedral and say prayers of thanks to the Lord, and to ask Him to keep us safe.

Marina didn't bring her diary, so she looked over my shoulder and continued to make suggestions as to what I should enter here. We just got silly and kept laughing until my mother reminded us again that we have to behave properly.

She didn't seem to be having such a good time. I don't know why, but my father was in high spirits, and teased her about being a stick-in-the-mud. Well, Marina and I got the message, and soon we went to bed.

The author interrupts once again to suggest that We follow the family around Ferrara and accompany them through the historic sights as part of their entourage. Since Gilda made no further entries, I'll take the liberty of suggesting what she would have written, if you can excuse the license.

Upon entering the Castello over one of the drawbridges and into the Courtyard, (Il Cortile) the family joined up with a group that was going to be guided through the Castello's Interior.

She let them through the main entrance and into a huge room that was once the reception room for the House of Este. Here she told of the meetings and parties that the room was used for, and which was also the scene of a swordfight involving many men.

We don't know what that fight was all about, but in any case, the d'Estes won, and the invaders all killed. The guide explained that some of the rooms on the first and second floors are now being used as government offices, and that the group must do everything they must not to disturb their work.

Senor Colonna commented that if they were government offices, the group would not have to worry about disturbing them because the chances were that they were not doing any work anyway. Everybody enjoyed a laugh at that, including the guide.

Senora Colonna was embarrassed and suggested to her husband that he should keep his comments to himself, since he himself was a government employee. The group laughed again, and that served to keep him quiet for the rest of the tour.

As the group waked on the guide told of Duke Ercole the First, who sired eight known children and many more outside of the Castello, since he was quite a womanizer.

Gilda whispered to Marina that she thought it was awful that the Duke cheated on his wife, but when Marina whispered back, asking Gilda what SHE would do, Gilda thought a moment and said that she would just let him do as he liked, she guessed.

Marina responded by saying that that was the sensible thing to do, men being what they are.

The guide said that when Alfonso the First became the new Duke, he and Lucrezia Borgia had six children. Gilda whispered to Marina that one of those children, Cardinal Ippolito, was the one who built the Villa d'Este at Tivoli.

Marina said that she already knew that because Gilda had told her several times already!

The Guide, continuing her talk while pretending not to notice the whispering between the girls, said that the Castello was originally built to protect the Estensi family from the mobs in the city. Times were hard, and the people were rioting.

Their mood was such that they grabbed the official they blamed for their troubles and literally tore him to pieces.

Inside the walls, the Castello was rebuilt and redesigned many times, with succeeding sections being more beautiful than the last. The Gothic rooms built by Nicolo the Second are the most beautiful.

The Castello's ravelins, those projections over the walls once used as defensive positions, were converted to kitchens for the preparation of food. It was a strange place for kitchens, but probable the best place considering that any other place would have been difficult and dangerous, considering the open fires.

The official who saw to the many needs of the Castello was called the "Scalco". It was he who also saw to the moving of whatever the family needed when they went to one of their summer places.

Then the group saw the prison room in which Alfonso threw his brother Giulio for plotting against him. Gilda and Marina agreed that it was a chilling place. After being led through a large galleria, we oversaw the loggia often used as a greenhouse, and the upper gardens of orange trees. What a wonderful aroma!

Then there is the room of Bacchus with paintings on the walls of that God, and Senor Colonna told the girls to close their eyes! Use your imagination! Well, in olden time sex was openly enjoyed. The author assumes you are familiar with the paintings found in the homes in Pompeii, and the Giuliano paintings in the Palazzo del Te.

In the Ducal chapel they saw the painted ceilings and the White Eagle of the Este. It is a small, rather plain room, but beautiful in is aspect.

Next, the Dawn Room is also called the room of mirrors. The paintings show the times of day, from dawn until the dark of night.

The little room of games followed then the room of poisons, which was the pharmacy of that time. It was so named because they made the poisons that were to be used against their enemies, but more about that is not known.

(Authors note: Lucrezia Borgia has sometime been called "The Poisoner", but after exhaustive research in the family archives and elsewhere, this appellation has been debunked. The Duchess was a very kind person, given to charity, and never harmed anyone.)

The Hall of games was used mostly to give concerts, but some indoor games were played here.

The room of the tower of Saint Catherine is also known as the room of patience, and is, oddly, decorated with the signs of the zodiac.

The antechamber to the Galleria displays the coats of arms of the Este. It also presents a good view of the towers of the Castello itself. The paintings show landscapes and naiads running around in the nude, as they were wont to do. Gilda and Marina looked wide-eyed at each other as if to say, "Oh, My!"

One wonders if Gilda's parent were beginning to regret this excursion. They were surprised by the nudity, but at least there were no scenes demonstrating the lust of the times. What would Marina say to HER parents?

The room of Hector shows a large map of the Duchy of the Este, including Modena and Reggio-Emelia. At one time the land owned and controlled by the Este family cut the peninsula of Italy in half.

(In my research I came across a piece that said the Adige River was named after the d'Este family, but I don't know how to verify that. The river flowed next to the fortress city of Este, where the family originated, and was at that time called the Ateste River. Author)

The Gallery Hall, the room of land reclamation, the Hall of Saint Paul's Tower, The Government antechamber, which is the room were people who wanted an audience with the Duke waited.

There followed Government Hall, where the Duke conducted the every day business of the running of the Duchy.

There is also the room with the sad name of Sala della Devoluzione, which shows the period when the Duke has to leave the Castello, and the Pope took over the Duchy of Ferrara.

Then the group entered the room of the landscapes, another Galleria, and the Sala delle Georgafie.

The Blue Salon, called the Council Room was not open to the group, but they peeked in anyway.

Finally, there is the room of the coat of arms. It is a large room well decorated with weapons and armor. Then the group was led down a fifteenth century spiral staircase that led back to the courtyard. The tour was over.

A lot more can be told about the Castello Estense in Ferrara, but this is a book about the Diary of Gilda Colonna. Perhaps some day the author will write more extensively on this imposing castle.

The next day the family visited both the Palazzo dei Diamante, which shows the Este Art collection., and the Palazzo Schiffanoia, a summer place for the Este family which is now used as a girl's school. Both buildings, as well as other properties once owned by the d'Este family are now under the umbrella of the Musei Civili d'Arte di Ferrara.

The Palazzo dei Diamante is so called because of the surface of the blocks on the outer walls being in the shape of "diamonds". It's a large building and its rooms are large, lending itself to many galleries and thus perfect for use as an art museum. It is the seat of the National Gallery of Art.

Unfortunately, recent management allowed the display of so called "modern art" which diminishes the original collection, in the opinion of this author. The display of this trash is supposed to enlighten, but its effect is to confirm the thinking of many aficionados that these works should rightly be consigned to the junk-heap of time.

Senor Colonna shook his head in disgust, but his wife had no comment. The girls tried to study these pieces, trying to understand what the artists meant in painting them, but of course, there is no real meaning to be found in them, and so the puzzle remains: Why display them?

Some argue that the artists wanted to express new ideas, being weary of the old school, but the truth may lie in the simple fact that the caliber of artists no longer exists in Italy. Then, if we care to look deeper, we may see evidence that there are nihilistic people who would like to see the true traditions destroyed. Your guess is as good as anyone's.

It is an easy walk from the Palazzo dei Diamante to the Palazzo Schiffanoia. In the latter Palazzo, the building has been almost totally stripped of its former glory. What was once a comfortable summer home for the d'Este family is now a girl's school. There is work being done to uncover and recover murals that were done by famous artists. The pity is that they were painted over with whitewash in the first place.

In my way of thinking, this shows a marked disrespect not only for the artwork, but for the history of my family as well. That this travesty should have been allowed is sad indeed. Now there is the painstaking job of recovering the precious art that was there and should have been left alone.

I beg the reader's pardon for going far afield. These sentiments were not entered in Gilda's diary, but who can say that Gilda did not have thoughts along these lines. She is an intelligent girl and has already shown a deep respect for the family of the House of Este.

Once their visit to the city of Ferrara was over, they took the train back to their home in Monza, and there remained only a few weeks before the girls were to prepare and leave for the University Bologna, where they were to start their studies anew.

In her diary she made reference to the trip, and indicated that she and Marina discussed the matter of Duke Ercole's infidelities, and what the modern wife should think about such things.

Gilda showed a surprising flexibility when she wrote:

Dear Diary,

I don't know if I would resent the infidelities of my future husband. I can think of more reasons to let it be, than to get into a lot of dissention over it. I see the boys in school paying attention to one girl, and the very next day acting like another was their one and only.

It may well be that this is their proper nature, despite the vows that are taken at the altar. Just as it is sad to see animals in the zoo being caged up, so it must be with men. They should not be expected to go against their own nature.

There is also the argument that if I think my husband is virile and attractive, why should I blame another woman for feeling the same way about him? Does this make sense?

Would I ask him to be unfaithful? No, I don't think so, yet might there not be certain extenuation circumstances wherein such a thing might not only present itself, but would be a kindness?

Just as we must recognize that a man may easily stray, then we can't deny that he will be with another woman, right? Might it not be true that this other woman, seeing his manliness, may choose him as the father of the child she her nature wants so much? Am I making sense?

Well, as usual, I have to sleep on this and discuss it with Marina tomorrow.

She may not be able to add anything to the discussion, but I heed my father when he says that two heads are better than one.

Dear Diary,

I think I confused Marina with my odd logic about husbands. She did not agree with me, but she did not disagree either. No doubt Marina will want a traditional marriage in which her man will not, or should not wander. Of course I would not exactly welcome infidelity. I'm only saying that if it is a fact, then accept it with grace..

With all this, there is not anything about me that's untraditional. I don't have wild ideas about politics or society. I obey my parents, and in fact I honor them, as the Commandments say I should.

I just have the feeling that husbands are another matter. My man will come to me as he is, and I do not have the talent to change him, I'm sure. Naturally I will do my best to hold his interest, but if I can't, then I feel it will be enough if he provides for any children we may have, and respects me enough as the woman he married.

Yes, that will be enough for me. I dare not discuss this subject with my parents. They would probably have me committed to a rubber room. No, they wouldn't do that, but they sure would worry.

If faced with such a reality, would my father challenge him to a duel? I think not, but one never knows about him. He's possessive and protective of his one and only girl.

Another thought is that maybe my husband will be one of those stick-in-the-mud types who would never stray, mostly because he never was lucky before marriage. Oh, my! How do I think of such things?

Dear Diary,

I must admit that it is hard to enter most of the things I've been doing these days. Life has become something of a bore while trying to pass the time before going to Bologna. Marina and Diana and I have been getting together, but we know that time will separate us, at least for the most part.

We renewed our vow to be friends always and to keep in touch in the many was we have of doing so. We can write letters and send notes and even telephone each other. I told Diana that she must tell us what she's learning in nursing school. I'm sure she will have an interesting life, although it promises to be hard.

Imagine looking after people who are sick or injured or very old. One must have the disposition for it and I'm surprised that Diana is sure she has. She never showed any interest in that before. She did say that she was not up to the courses of study at the University, though.

I think she should have tried. It's possible that her family could not afford to send her, but she said nothing about that. She would have been too proud to admit that, Of course, I'm just speculating.

It's not as though Marina and I think it's going to be a piece of cake. Senora Danno said it was not going to be easy, and judging by our last year in second level, this warning might have scared Diana off. I almost did Marina and me.

Dear Diary,

In just a few more days my life will change forever. I've got all my clothes and other things to take to the university, and I even have the notice telling us what rooms we have been assigned to. Marina and I will not even be in the same dorm. I don't know how they decide these things, but I'll be going to her dorm to see her often.

I'm still going to pursue my interest in Psychology, but I won't have courses in that until the second year. I understand that the first year is mostly for general learning and in experimental matters. I'm not sure what all that means, but I'll know soon enough.

This means that I'll have a roommate that I don't know. I can only hope I don't get a bad one. Not many girls are raised as I have been, with strict guidelines to live by. Too many girls are too loose in their ways. I don't mean they are bad. They are just loose in their beliefs and behavior.

My mother told me to be wary of girls that seem to tolerate too much. She warns that these girls set the wrong example, and I am not to be persuaded by them. I certainly intend to live by that. I'll hold to my core beliefs and no one will change that, even if they poke fun at me.

Marina promises to do the same. We'll support each other. My father gave me a speech, but I couldn't help thinking of how easy it is for girls to frustrate their father's wishes.

For brevity, the author takes this opportunity to condense all the pages in the diary that describe the University of Bologna. The full name is: Alma Mater Studiorum Universita di Bologna, UNIBO.

It is the oldest continually operating degree-granting university in the world. This institution at its foundation in about 1088 first used the very word "University". It is ranked as one of the top 50 of the world's universities.

It has twenty three faculties, and has about 90,000 students. It's going to be easy for our Gilda to feel lost there, where Dante Alighieri and Francesco Petrarca studied.

Nicolaus Copernicus, Albrecht Durer and the unfortunate poet Torquato Tasso studied here. Tasso was imprisoned for most of his life in a cellar dungeon for making ovations of love to Leonora d'Este at the Castello Estense in Ferrara. While incarcerated, he went mad.

(Leonora went on to marry the Prince of Verona.)

Senor Colonna drove his daughter and her friend Marino to the university, along with Marina's father, who came to see that his daughter was properly settled in. All of them were awed by the size of the campus, and the many buildings it comprised.

Gilda went to her dorm first, and her father saw to her settlement. Then he drove Marina and her father to her dorm, and waited until her father came back to the car. Both fathers were teary-eyed, and decided to go somewhere for a drink or two.

Italian fathers are all right when it comes to their sons being liberated, but they are nearly broken-hearted when their daughters grow up. Is this heard to understand? They seem to think of their daughters as dolls who are supposed to stay forever young and safe, and to enjoy their parent's company for all of their days.

When their girls grow up, Italian fathers are usually taken by surprise. They wonder who this woman is in their households. Believe me; it sometimes causes a lot of dissention between the father and the mother, who has to convince him to give the girl more freedom.

Then when the girls go off to the university, they feel abandoned and betrayed. Read what happened to this author and his eldest daughter when SHE announced that she wanted to become a NUN, in the book "An American Duke in Italy".

When a girl starts puberty and her hormones bring to about obvious changes, fathers refuse to notice, but let a boy who noticed come calling for her and watch the fur fly. How often have fathers accused their innocent daughters of seductively flaunting their charms?

Ask a father of a mature daughter if it is easier to raise girls or boys. He'll say boys are less worry, but the truth is that girls are more obedient and caring. It's the father who is the problem. He goes nuts when he finally realizes that his daughter has become a woman. Tell him he has to let go, and he'll show his fangs.

Perhaps the question should be: Which is the easier parent, the father or the mother?

During the first two years of her studies at the University of Bologna, Gilda all but forgot about here diary, and who could blame her. The workload was very heavy, and she had the naïveté to think that she had to study every page of her books, not noticing that her fellow students found a way around that.

She had learned that one of the math teachers Marina was studying under was a Professoressa Beatrice d'Este, daughter of the Duke of Este. She was enthralled by this but the opportunity to meet her didn't present itself right away..

When she was in her third year, she was still working hard, accepting it all as her obligation to herself, her parents and the university. Then something happened to turn her life topsy-turvy.

The Professoressa Beatrice d'Este came to find HER! She was absolutely thrilled by this attention until Beatrice told her why she came to search her out.

Her father, the Duke, had asked her to find out about one Gilda Colonna, a psychology student at the university. Gilda did not understand why this was happening. She asked why the Duke should be interested in HER.

That's when she was told that she was being considered for a contracted marriage to the Duke's nephew, Antonino Vincenti "Vince" d'Este, who was being groomed to be the next Duke.

Gilda was too shocked to ask how this all came about. She could not have known that it was her father who contacted the Duke when he learned that a bride was being sought for his nephew.

Gilda was near tears when she understood what all this purported to mean. If the families could agree on the terms of a contract, she would marry Vince shortly after her graduation from the university. It was as simple as that!

She begged for answers about this Vince, but Beatrice could not give her any information about him because, even though he was her cousin, she had never met him. All she could supply by way of making things clearer was that Vince was an American.

Oh no! Oh Lord! Not an American! She could not think! This could not be happening.

She begged Beatrice to get more information. Q. Will she be able to finish school? A. Yes she would! Q. What about her profession as a Psychologist? That had no answer. Q. Where would she live, in America? A. No, in the Castello Estense, know as the Castello Laura, among other names.

Q. Where was that? A. Near the city of Monza, about twenty kilometers east of there. Q. I'm from there, how come I never heard of it? A. It's a very private home, not like other castles in Italy. Q. Who lives there? A. I did, until I came here. And so it went, the confused Gilda is trying her best to understand.

Beatrice was not being very understanding of the Girl's state of mind. She just patiently answered whatever questions she could, but did not offer any sort of consolation, not even when Gilda burst into tears.

Beatrice left the frightened girl to fend for herself, and the first thing that came to Gilda's mind was to run and see Marina. She thought of calling her parents, but hesitated. After all, it was her father who had to be arraigning this. Who else?

She didn't find Marina right away and was in a near panic without someone to talk to. When she saw Marina in an auditorium, she screamed her name, and all the people there thought she had gone insane.

Marina ran to her, now in a near panic herself, to find out what the matter was. In the hallway, Gilda poured out the problem, and Marina could not believe any of it. It sounded like a fairy tale, but they both knew that Beatrice d'Este would not lie about anything.

Marina had to go beck to the auditorium, so Gilda called her father and repeated what Beatrice told her. Her father affirmed what she was told, and then informed her as to how it all came about.

Gilda asked what Vince was like, and her father repeated what he was told; that Vince was a rough man who was working as a Bounty Hunter, but that he came from a good family, and was the nephew of the reigning Duke. He was a talented tennis player, having won the New York State Championship a few years ago. Further, he shows good manners and is very intelligent.

She asked if she was ready for this, and was assured that the marriage would not take place until after she graduated. There was time for her to meet him, and get used to the idea.

Gilda was still in a daze and asked to speak to her mother. This time she got the love and nurturing she needed to blunt the shock of suddenly finding herself being contracted to marry a man from a distant land.

He mother was very reassuring, even though she herself was in a dazed state. She and her daughter prayed together over the phone asking the Lord to make sure everything would be all right.

Afterward, Gilda asked to be excused from classes for the rest of the day, and when her fellow students learned why, the flocked around her. All were congratulatory, and that made Gilda begin to feel like some kind of a star.

Later, Marina said it was so fantastic to think Gilda would become the Duchess of Este. Gradually, Gilda began to lose some of her trepidation and began to think it was a miracle, and answer to her prayer to become a great lady.

She imagined herself to be like Lucrezia d'Este Borgia, sweet and generous to all "her" people. Now she had to meet the rough man. She prayed for strength. She was still a child, with no experience that may have helped an older woman to weather the surprise.

Then she began to feel a new fear. Suppose HE didn't like ME? Just like any young girl, she began to swing from one fear to another. First she feared marrying the man, and then she feared NOT marrying him.

It's amazing how females can run themselves through the gamut of emotion on the very same topic. Men seem to be immune from that. Gilda did not know what to do with herself, so she went to her dorm room and fell on her bed and cried; racking sobs that had to come out of her if she were not to bottle it all up inside.

He roommate, Veronique, did not know what to say until Marina came over, and the three of them discussed it into the wee hours of the morning. It was necessary, but it meant that the next day they were all bleary-eyed, and their concentration suffered.

Gilda's roommate was more experienced in worldly matters, or perhaps we should say she was less naïve. She felt quite strongly that Gilda was very fortunate to be able to gain even a foothold in the House of Este. It would mean that she would be set for the rest of her life.

It was Veronique who would be chosen as Gilda's Maid of Honor at her wedding. She had Aristocratic credentials.

Marina was thinking with her heart, however, and she felt that her dear friend Gilda could be heading into a lot of trouble being married to a rough man. There's no telling but that he may harm her in the future, she said.

The roommate said however, that such a man would be worth paying any price to marry. She asked the other girls how many men were available with such position and qualities that he possessed.

Dear Diary,

I apologize once again for neglecting your pages for so long, but you'll understand when I tell you that I'm being contracted to marry an American. Last night I heard he was coming to Italy, and that he will want to meet ME. This is something I must face by myself, but I wish I could send a stand-in.

Actually, what do I have to fear? He can come to my house and my parents will be there to manage things. After all, he's a man, not a hungry tiger. He will be on his best behavior, and no one will have to fight him, I don't think.

Oh, Lord! Marriage! I'm not ready for this. How can I learn everything? Can my mother teach me all the things I'll need to know? I can hardly cook.

They must have people who do cooking and cleaning in the House of Este. Of course they do! Why am I dwelling on such silly things? He's only a man! My mother manages my father very well! Oh, yes! I've seen how she does it. She's very subtle about it.

Then again, he loves her. If my husband doesn't love me, I won't be able to manage him. How terrible all this is! Maybe my life is going to be a total ruin. Wait! I can ask Marina to come and live with me as my companion. Great ladies have companions. I know that much.

No, I can't ask her to do that. She has to live HER life too. I must sleep. My mind is running around in little circles. In class I learned that no one ever knows his own mind. This proves it!

Dear Diary,

He's in Italy, and he's going to meet my parents. Will he come to the university? I hope not! Perhaps my parents will show him some photographs of me, and maybe he'll be satisfied with those.

No, he won't be! He'll want to talk to me. What will I say to him? Lord, how do I talk to such a man? I'll make sure Marina is with me. She can help with the conversation. Maybe he won't do any of these things. I'll just wait and see. I must study. I fear my grades will suffer now.

I wish it were all over somehow. I see now that it's not easy being a girl. Boys don't worry as much as girls do. I wonder why that is. They are always so sure of themselves, the brutes!

Tomorrow I'll call home and see what's happening. He may just take his sweet time in getting around to me. That would be just like a man! They don't mind when we wait and lose our patience.

No, he wouldn't want to wait. Men have sex on their minds all the time, and they are always in hot pursuit. That's what Veronique said, but Marina disagrees with that. She says that she hasn't noticed any of the boys being in hot pursuit of HER!

Just because she doesn't notice it doesn't mean they are not, Veronique said.

She's pretty enough, and I'll bet they are, but they are being sneaky about it, then, before she knows what's happening, they'll steal a kiss, right on her lips, too. That's where they like to kiss girls, the sneaks!

What if Vince wants to kiss me on the lips? If we are contracted to marry, does he have the right to do that? I'll ask my mother.

Dear Diary,

He has visited my parents, and he said he's coming to the university tomorrow. My mother says he's a handsome man, and very polite. Maybe I'll like him too. Maybe I'll let him kiss me on the lips.

Even if he's polite to my parents, he may want to do more with me. Suppose he's the kind of man that likes to put his hand up girl's dresses! I can't let him do that. Marina must be with me at all times.

I'm feeling very tense. I think my father should have waited until I was older to match me with a grown man. If he wants to put his hand up my dress, I'd better be sure I have my best underwear on. He would be very rude to do that, but if he does, what would I be able to do to stop him.

What would it be like having him touch my underwear? It may tickle! I must stop thinking about it. I think I'm committing a sin thinking about all this, but if he touches my underwear, it won't be MY fault. It will be HIS sin, and he must confess it to the priest.

He will do that when we are married, so maybe it won't be so bad if he did it now. Well, if he does, I won't like it, and I'll insist that he stop it. I'll let him touch me for just a minute, and then I'll tell him to stop.

I'd better not say this to Marina or Veronique. They will surely think I'm willing to encourage that kind of behavior with the man I'm to marry. Well, if there will be an agreement on a contract, that is.

Suppose they can't agree on the contract terms. What will I do for a husband then?

Dear Diary,

I'm totally disgusted with this brute that I've been considered for marriage. He came to the university, and in the parking lot he smashed a student's face in with his fist. What kind of savage do they expect to contract me to? I will not marry such a barbarian.

It seems that Americans always want to get into fights. Everywhere they go there's trouble. If this is the kind of man I must consider, then I may not get married at all.

The Professoressa Beatrice d'Este came to see me. She's very angry that Vince punched that student, especially on the university grounds. She told me that she will oppose the marriage, and that she will try to get her father to recall Vince back to the United States.

For a few brief days I was happy that I was going to marry a strong man, but now I see that Marina was right. He may hurt me some day in the future, No, marriage to Vince d'Este is out of the question, and I shall tell my father so.

I know that I cannot be forced to marry him, so I need not trouble my mind with all this any longer. I'm free to continue my studies with a clear mind.

Oh dear! I think I want him. I'm told that the poor man has broken his hand and has needed surgery. A broken hand must be very painful, and all wrapped up in a cast must be very uncomfortable. I wish I could console him. Still it's his very own fault! He broke the student's face, and the student will need surgery too.

Dear Dairy.

I didn't' get to meet Vince after all. After he was treated at the hospital, he went back to the Castello Laura. When I told my father I didn't think I should marry him my father said that that was nonsense, and that the incident only proved that Vince d'Este was a strong man.

He told me that people are applauding him and turning him into a hero for some reason. I can't understand that. He behaved like a thug, but people are saying that the student asked for it. Even the student admitted he was in the wrong when a witness came forward and told what happened.

Still I will not marry him if only because I want to so much. At first my friends thought I was crazy, but then they began to say that they understood what I meant by that. I simply must take my time and think things over very carefully. A girl can't be too cautious. After the marriage it will be too late.

Will he call me or write me a letter? I think he owes me that much. He must appreciate that he has left a girl waiting, and he must make up for that. If I am to be a great lady, I must begin now by insisting that he treat me like one.

What will happen now? The waiting will surely kill me! Men! They do drive us crazy. They really do!

I must take my mind of this situation, yet, how can I? This is such an important moment in my life. How can I just ignore it?

What do great ladies do? I'll go to the library and see if I can find something on this subject. Beatrice won't tell me. Maybe my mother can.

Dear Dairy.

I've been told that Vince is flying back to the United States to get a specialist to see about his broken hand. I fear he will be away for weeks. My father said that the contract will go forward, and that I must not behave in an unappreciative way.

I told him that I would obey him, but that I naturally had reservations about marrying a brutal man. He though that was funny! He made it very clear that I would be well treated and happy as the Duchess of the House of Este. I suppose he's right. Certainly my friends think so.

One thing that Vince succeeded in doing was making an enemy of Beatrice. She was so embarrassed by his behavior in the parking lot that she took a leave of absence and went home to the Castello Laura.

I have not been able to follow anything else about the d'Este family, since they tend to be very private people, and I was hoping my father could get some news about Vince, but he had no information either.

Now I feel that I am in limbo. I am not able to concentrate on my studies as before, nor am I able to hope for my future with an exciting husband, and the life of a great lady. My appetite is gone and not even a feast would make me want to eat.

The only happiness I want now it to be in bed with a husband I have never seen, and who gives me strange thrills at the thought of his caressing me. I fear I am lost in a trap not of my making. What does a woman do in such circumstances?

The author interrupts again. I'm sure the reader has noticed how our Gilda has changed from a girl who obeyed her parents and the religious thinking about proper behavior, and who listened carefully to words about avoiding sin, to a woman who is listening to the calls of her own nature.

For the first time in her diary she refers to herself as a woman. She has moved away from her suspicion of the motives of boys, to the desire to merge in concupiscent completion with "her" husband.

We cannot say that this transformation is sudden. No, rather, it is in the hearts and minds of every natural female, and, like a simple flower in the field, blossoms as soon as the sun shines its light and warmth on it. She may not realize its reality, but all of it is designed to point in only one direction. It is the path to motherhood.

Nature wants babies; that's all there is to that. The young man, whose hormones are demanding that he pump his "swimmers" into the dark recesses of a woman's body, is only obeying the force of creation. He wants HIS seed to populate the world, This is known as the Gene-pool imperative.

The young woman also feels that force, and somehow knows that she will open her body to invite the one man her heart has locked upon. He is the man of her dreams, and like our Gilda, she doesn't even have to see him. His image is stamped in her mind, and she is ready to take him in.

One of the saddest things in human life happens when this natural process is corrupted.

Let us not forget that our Gilda is still quite young, as you will see as we sneakily read the pages of her diary once again.

.

Dear Diary,

I don't want to think about the time it has taken for my Vince to come back to Italy. Now he's back at the Castello Laura, and we, my parents and I, have been invited to dinner there. I will see the Castello for the first time, and finally meet the man I love.

What shall I wear? What shall I say to him? I must find the right words so that he doesn't think I'm a dunce. He's a man of the world, and I feel like a feather in the wind. What is clear to me is that I have not been prepared for this moment. Is a woman ever prepared?

Some women seem to be. I think I have to be more of a free spirit now. I wonder if religion retards a woman's nature, or does it prepare her for her natural role in life. I can't seem to come to any conclusion about this.

One would think that all my studies on the human mind would suffice to make me feel like I was on more solid ground, but somehow none of that is working for me. I'm all at sea! A man of my own! Imagine!

Oh, how silly of me. There isn't even a contract yet and I'm running ahead of the facts. I'd better be prepared for the eventuality of a failure in this arrangement. We can't assume it will work. It isn't THAT easy to gain entry into to House of Este.

I'm going to pray now so that God and Mother Mary will intercede for me, so that I may, through this marriage, do His temporal work.

Dear Diary,

He likes me! When he showed me around the huge room called the Crystal Room, we sat on a settee, and he kissed me. He kissed me right on the lips. I think he furtively passed his had over one of my breasts too. I think so because I felt a very strong thrill in the nipple.

He then took me into the chapel but he didn't cross himself with holy water as we entered. He walked me up and down the center aisle, then we looked at all the Stations of the Cross, but he didn't genuflect when we crossed before the altar. I don't think Vince is religious.

I will tell my parents about this. They may think it's a bad sign. I must have looked a little flushed from that kiss because I saw my parents look at each other. Could they tell? What did that look signify?

There is so much to life that it's no wonder people, especially the young, are so confused. I can't understand what's happening to my own body. When I think of the caress of my breast, I get a strange sensation in my nipples. I even think of asking Vince to do it again, but I dare not actually do that.

I caressed them during my bath, and they rose up, but that's a sin, and anyway, it's different when Vince does it, I think. I would like him to do it again.

I love him. He IS strange, but I do love him so, and I think I will die if I can't marry him. Well, die in spirit anyway. If only you could talk, diary! What would you tell me?

Dear Diary,

The dinner at the Castello was excellent. I don't remember when I enjoyed my food more. Vince saw us to our car and I wanted so much to stay with him. After we got home, my father asked me so many questions that I felt like I ws getting the third degree, but he was being kindly, and I answered as best as I can.

I told my father I wanted to marry him, and he was pleased to hear that. He pointed out the magnificence of the Castello, and the obvious fact that I would live as a Duchess should. He didn't have to tell me that, but it was Vince I wanted, and would have taken him if he were a common man

That doesn't make sense! He's certainly not a common man!

Anyway, my father said that the contract will go forward, and there will be a slight delay as the finer points are ironed out, but that he was confident that he would have an iron-clad document soon.

I will be going back to school tomorrow, and can't wait to tell Marina and my roommate what happened. I can predict that Marina will be amazed, but my roommate has been kissing boys on the lips for some time, and has even been what she called. "Felt up!"

My roommate is not a bad girl, but she was raised in different circumstances and has had experiences that Marina and I did not. She understood, and never laughed at us for being naïve, but she didn't hesitate to correct us about certain things involving men.

Dear diary,

We have a contract! It has been approved by both families and seems to be equitable for all concerned. The wedding is to take place soon after my graduation from the university.

Word has gotten around the university that I am to be the new Duchess of the House of Este, and my popularity is greater than ever. I'm happy to say that Marina is not jealous and is very supportive. I told her that I want her and Diana to be my friends forever, no matter what happens. I have their assurance that they will be.

Do I have to say how dizzy all this is making me? I must study to pass my exams, and I cannot use these developments as an excuse for neglecting my lessons or my homework. I must remember that I have a career to think about, and I want to set up my office before we start having any babies.

I don't think it's wrong for a Duchess to have a professional career. Why should that be a problem? I like all the things I have learned, and I want to be able to practice my profession and help many people solve their personal problems. It's a wonderful thing.

I wonder what my man is doing now. He will have a lot of work once he becomes the new Duke, but right now he has enough free time to think of ME! He must be thinking about me. After all, he kissed me on the lips soon after I met him!

Vince d'Este! I'm going to be sleeping with him and I will fly among the stars. I'm sure.

Author: The entries in the diary become repetitive so I'll skip most of them and tell of certain events that were markedly different. Vince visited the university again and this time was guided to her classroom.

Gilda was surprised and blushed hotly while the class gaped at the man who was to be her husband and the new Duke of Este. The teacher dismissed the class early and there was a momentary bedlam in the room while the girls gathered around the couple, and the boys just gaped at the scene.

Later, the couple had lunch and then walked around the campus with a bevy of girls in tow. They had to answer many questions, but could not give complete answers to some because there was much about the future they didn't know.

When Gilda graduated she put on her graduation ring on her third finger of her left hand, but it didn't stay there long. As part of the preparations for the wedding, Gilda and her parents moved into the Castello Laura for convenience.

They were married in the Cathedral at Monza with a lot less fuss than when Laura was married, and there was a reception in a hall in Monza, and then a family reception in the Crystal Room in the Castello.

Among the many dignitaries was the Prince Pallavicino with his wife, the Princess Tinti, and Prince von Pappen with his daughter the Princess Helga, who was Laura's Maid-of-Honor.

Gilda's Maid-of-Honor was her dear friend and roommate a t the university Veronique, and Marina and Diana were bridesmaids.

The couple went to start their honeymoon in the Palazzo d'Este in Milano. A few nights later Gilda wrote:
Dear Diary,

I do not have the words to describe our wedding night. My husband was gentle, but I still had the sensation that he was going to split me open. He kept filling me more and more and I wondered just how large a man gets during the marriage act.

I had to tell him he was hurting me, but after he was finished, he kissed me gently then slept for a while. In about an hour he wanted to take me again, but I told him I felt sore there. He ignored my protests and took me for the second time and oh my God! This time my body responded with the most unbelievable sensations!

The ecstatic waves washed over me again and again, and I didn't want him to stop. That such a thing could happen to a woman explains why they are so willing to submit to men. Soreness or not, I must have more of this.

We will be going to the United States, specifically to New York and then to a place up north called Niagara Falls. After that we'll go to visit His Grace Antonino in Florida.

During our honeymoon I discovered a few things about myself. One was that I could be a coward under certain circumstances. I was afraid to go under the falls in Niagara. The falls were indeed frightening.

Then I discovered that I was a true chiacarone. When we got to Florida I told His Grace Antonino how virile my husband was. Vince complained that his uncle did not have to know everything.

It was nice in Florida, and I can see why His Grace Antonino chose to live there.

Dear Diary,

When we finally got home to the Castello, people were addressing me as "Your Grace", and I was surprised to hear that. It took a while for me to realize that while I might think of myself as a great lady, I was not going to live like Lucrezia d'Este Borgia.

No, I was going to stay at home and simply attend to the needs of daily life in the Castello. And what became of my dream to start a professional practice? The dream was gone when I found myself to be pregnant.

That may have changed my ideas for the future, but my being a chiacarone didn't change. I told Leonora, Regina and others there how "forte" my husband was in bed. Regina was affected by this and asked me if she could have Vince.

Now, I ask you, diary, how could I refuse her I was having morning sickness, and my husband was always fired up and ready to roll in the "sack", he would call it.

Regina needed love, so with my permission she took Vince to her, and my Italian Stallion soon had HER with child.

My morning sickness was severe and I was forced to stay in bed much of the time. Later I learned that Vince had impregnated Deli, a dancer before we were married. She was a Syrian girl who lived with the family. He then wanted to bed Leonora, but she refused, at first.

Some time later, when Leonora's husband proved to be impotent, she lay with Vince and got pregnant too.

My husband seemed to be satisfied after that, and settled down to his family work. He occasionally "bounces

Deli and Regina, but otherwise his extra-curricular days seem to be over.

Author: When Gilda was asked how she could tolerate her husband's infidelities, she asked simply, "When you own a wild stallion, what can you do with such an animal? You let him run until he gets tired. That's what I did, and it worked."

Smart lady, wouldn't' you say?

Afterward: Gilda delivered a baby girl, as she said she would, and named it Maria, after her mother. Regina had another boy, and Deli also had a boy. Leonora delivered a girl.

Despite the fact that all of the children resembled Vince, no one said a word, and so life went on somewhat normally in the Castello Laura.

Gilda's second baby was a much wanted boy, who was named Piero III, after Vince's father. Vince's pride was evident when everyone saw that he took the boy everywhere with him. As the years went by, little Piero showed every sign that he was going to be like his father.

His intelligence and fearlessness was noted, and no one messed with him. He knew he would be the next Duke, and acted like it. The child also developed a love for the land.

Gilda's friend Marina went on to become a teacher, and was working in the same school the three friends went to in Monza.

Gilda continued to make entries into her diary, but we don't have to read further. We know what she was writing there now, don't we?

The end, or is it just the beginning?

Antonino Vincenti d'Este